DEPENDING ON STRANGERS

DEPENDING ON STRANGERS
Freedom, Memory and the Unknown Self

David P. Levine

PHOENIX
PUBLISHING HOUSE
firing the mind

First published in 2021 by
Phoenix Publishing House Ltd
62 Bucknell Road
Bicester
Oxfordshire OX26 2DS

British Library Cataloguing in Publication Data

A C.I.P. for this book is available from the British Library

ISBN-13: 978-1-912691-89-0

Typeset by Medlar Publishing Solutions Pvt Ltd, India

www.firingthemind.com

Contents

Part II
Concern for the welfare of others

About the author

David Levine is emeritus professor in the Josef Korbel School of International Studies at the University of Denver. He holds a PhD in economics from Yale University and a Certificate in Psychoanalytic Scholarship from the Colorado Center for Psychoanalytic Studies. He has published extensively in the fields of economics, political economy, political theory, and applied psychoanalysis. His most recent work includes: *Psychoanalysis, Society, and the Inner World* (2017), *Dark Fantasy* (2018), and *The Destroyed World and the Guilty Self* (with Matthew Bowker, 2019).

Introduction

This book was completed during the early stages of the Covid-19 pandemic. The pandemic radically altered people's lives along a number of significant dimensions. Among these, one of the most important was a widespread increase in the anxiety associated with tasks that made up everyday life. Thus, to take one important example, trips to the grocery store that are, by their nature, filled with casual contact with strangers became potentially fatal encounters with people who could transmit a deadly disease. The pursuit of the things we needed to sustain our lives was now a life-threatening activity. When our sustenance depends on strangers, it depends on trust in strangers. The pandemic challenged the links of trust between people and therefore undermined their confidence that they could safely interact with and even depend on one another.

Beyond the matter of becoming infected, the adverse impact of the pandemic on the availability of some of the goods needed for everyday life, due in large part to hoarding prompted by anxiety, undermined the conviction that our well-being is secure when we depend on strangers to provide us with the things we need. Anxiety about the availability of the things we need prompts an urge to hoard, an urge that can be both shared by others and projected onto them. The result is to create the shortages hoarding is meant to protect against and transform strangers into competitors for scarce goods.

This situation puts the "goods" over which we compete with strangers and the danger of infection they pose into a clearer light. Strangers can become the incarnation of loss or absence of care (strangers do not care about us) and the source of a life-destroying infection, both literally and symbolically. The good that is lost is the good (safe) feeling about the self that depends on the availability of emotional nutrients in the form of affirmation of our presence by others. The virus can come to represent the external shape of an internal aggression mounted against the self. The internal aggressor is projected onto those perceived to be our competitors over scarce goods. These goods in the external world also represent those things possession of which makes us a locus of the good self so that our inability to possess them becomes a sign that we have an impaired or bad self, which is a self unable to care for itself and unworthy to receive the care of others.

One way of coping with this situation is what Donald Winnicott refers to as "hiding" the self (1965, p. 46). During the pandemic, hiding the self took the tangible form of retreating into our homes and keeping strangers out. Strangers, then, are used to contain both our own loss of contact with ourselves and our own aggression against the self, which is held responsible for that loss.

The threat posed by others, however reality based it might be, has now formed a connection with an internal threat and, as a consequence, there develops an impulse to substitute the latter for the former in coping with the danger. Once others have come to occupy a place in our inner world, we are no longer indifferent to them; they have come to *matter* to us. But the movement away from indifference need not be a movement in the direction of a positively invested emotional connection but instead toward hostility born of the danger they are perceived or imagined to pose. To matter to another may mean to be loved by them, but it can also mean to be distrusted, even hated, by them.

In a world where livelihood depends on exchange, we depend on strangers. We depend on strangers because we have a significant degree of separation from the groups on which we depended before they were displaced by systems of private transactions. As a result of this displacement, our sustenance is no longer secured by our group attachment.

In the individual life, this separation from the group is enacted first as a separation from our family of origin. Separation from the family leaves us on our own in a world of people we must depend on without the kind of trust in dependence we had when we were growing up. Put in another language, strangers do not have the obligation of care family members did, so that, to some important extent, we now must find a way to care for ourselves, most notably through entering into the kinds of relations with strangers through which we acquire what we need from them not because they care about us, but because we can make use of each other without caring.

Group dependence also differs from dependence on strangers in that, while the former implies sharing a group identity that is defined externally to the individual, the latter does not. Groups significantly limit the space allowed in our lives for a personal sense of who we are. Put another way, the group is not a space in which a connection to what is uniquely personal about us—the self—can safely be made. Because of this, freedom means a significant degree of separation from the group and therefore a significant measure of dependence on strangers. This dependence extends beyond the market and applies even where dependence is on public institutions. Public institutions are not groups to which we belong; they are not friends or family. The eclipse of the group as the setting for need satisfaction means that where we cannot depend on the market, neither do we have recourse to groups as an alternative. Rather, dependence on strangers becomes the rule.

Freedom, then, requires that we have the emotional capacity to engage with and depend on strangers. When strangers provoke anxiety, our ability to depend on them is undermined. Because, in a market-centered economy, self-reliance means managing relations with strangers, by undermining our ability to depend on strangers, stranger anxiety undermines our capacity for self-reliance. Stranger anxiety is an emotional interpretation of others. The foundation for this emotional interpretation is set early in life through internalization of relations with caregivers. The emotional information contained in the internalization guides us in negotiating relationships with those outside the family.

More specifically, the stronger the basis for trust established early on, the less anxiety will be built into our interpretation of strangers; and conversely, the weaker the foundation of trust established early in our lives, the more our emotional interpretation of strangers will take the form of anxiety.

Our emotional interpretation of strangers, especially our interpretation of their reliability as sources of sustenance, is bound up with our trust in ourselves. Trust in ourselves refers first to our capacity to enter into a deliberative process likely to produce solutions to problems, including those signaled by anxiety, and second on our ability to act on those solutions. Both moments are important. The second moment—the ability to act on our decisions—depends on the instantiation in the mind of memories and fantasies of experiences in which what we did made a difference, most notably in commanding the attention of others, attention that affirmed our presence and its significance to them. This is vital to living in a world marked by dependence on strangers because it establishes, as a core element of our inner worlds, the conviction and expectation that our need, once clearly expressed, will be responded to in a positive way. Thus, memory, freedom, and the ability to live with strangers are bound together in a single emotional reality.

* * *

If we were to attempt to identify the quality of the contemporary world that poses the greatest emotional challenge to those who must live in it, it might be the necessity just considered of living with and depending on people we do not know and who do not know us. The necessity of living with people we do not know requires that we live a significant part of our lives outside the sphere of family and friends: in "society." In this book, I explore both the emotional burden we experience living with people we do not know and the unique opportunity doing so affords. While our emotional struggles are not all derived from this necessity, many are, and those that are have special importance when we focus our attention on the interplay between the inner world and the world outside.

In understanding both the opportunity and the emotional burden of living in society, the term freedom is of special importance. Here, I use that term to refer to the opportunity to escape, or negate, predetermination of our lives, by which I have in mind determination of how we live and experience our lives independently of our presence in them. Freedom is absent in our lives when we live exclusively with people who have a claim to prior knowledge of who we are and can impose that knowledge on us. But the matter of freedom does not end in the world of relating to others; it also has its place in the inner world: the world of thoughts and ideas. Knowing and not knowing, being known and not being known, all engage the matter of the free movement of thoughts and ideas as an internal matter.

Free movement of thoughts and ideas is one dimension or moment of freedom, the one we refer to as "inner freedom." But inner freedom cannot sustain itself on its own. For inner freedom there must also be two other dimensions: freedom to relate, which is also the freedom not to relate, and freedom in relating, which is the possibility of maintaining secure self-boundaries in relating to others. In this book I explore the reality of freedom, which is the integration of its three moments.

The free movement of thoughts and ideas is a vital part of the activity we refer to when we speak of "introspection." Distrust of introspection is common in the world in which many of us live. Distrust of introspection means distrust of the urge to inhabit a private world, a world kept safe from the unwanted intrusions, or, in Donald Winnicott's term, "impingements," of others (Levine, 2017). Distrust of introspection is, then, closely linked to distrust of an inner world that only those we invite are allowed to share with us.

As Heinz Kohut (1982) reminds us, psychoanalysis is a special form or method of introspection. It follows that, where introspection is viewed with distrust and even hostility, psychoanalysis will also be viewed that way as will the psychoanalytic study of society. One way to think about the end or purpose of psychoanalysis is to think about a way of being and living that emerges out of the exercise of the ability to negate or turn away from the external world so that the inner world can be fully experienced and known.

Doing so can be considered an end in itself. But it also opens up the possibility of engaging the world outside on a new and different basis, one in which a particular kind of internal experience shapes doing and relating. Coming to know the inner world is an ongoing process. It is not, then, only knowing the inner world that is the goal but the process of coming to know that world. The end of psychoanalysis can, then, be considered the internalization of a process the ongoing nature of which alters the experience both of self and of others. I take this to be the intent of those psychoanalytic ideas and methods that emphasize object relations and especially the shape of the internal object world. My purpose in this book is to make use of psychoanalytic ideas to further our understanding of the meaning and possibility of freedom, to understand better what freedom is and why it matters.

Consideration of the importance of introspection can also highlight the importance of certain norms of living typical in contemporary society. These are norms of privacy that, on the societal level, protect the integrity of the inner world. Notable among these are the private spaces in which we live: our homes. Private space mirrors or reproduces the privacy of the inner world in the physical reality of the world outside. None of this diminishes the importance of relating to others, but only highlights the importance of assuring that relating expresses, so far as possible, the individual's "freedom to relate" as Roger Kennedy (1993) so aptly terms it.

So far as the capacity to relate to strangers is poorly developed or impaired to some significant degree, encounters with people not known to us create anxiety and carry the potential for violation of boundaries and therefore also of norms of privacy. In this way, impairment in the capacity to live with strangers undermines respect for the privacy and autonomy of others. In the limit, this can lead to various forms and degrees of violation of rights including assault. Anxiety about living with strangers can drive people away from others. It can sponsor a powerful impulse to insist that strangers are not strangers at all but already well known to us as emanations of our inner worlds (internal object relations). And it can foster attacks on those we experience as strangers aimed at resolving our anxiety by eliminating what we imagine to be its source.

Part I

Freedom and memory

CHAPTER 1

Freedom

Predetermination

In his book, *Forces of Destiny*, Christopher Bollas explores the significance of unique presence or personal idiom in the human experience. In his understanding, each of us has "a set of unique person possibilities … subject in its articulation to the nature of lived experience in the actual world" (1989, p. 9). For there to be a personal idiom, the trajectory of life must not be preordained, but must be, at least along some vital dimension, yet to be determined. He uses the term fate to refer to a life the trajectory of which is preordained by forces outside the individual, and the term destiny for a life trajectory that emerges out of the urge "to establish oneself" (p. 33).

Bollas speaks of a "sense of destiny" by which he has in mind "the parts of the self that have not been split off and remain 'inside' the subject, giving him a sense of being on the right track" (p. 33). Following one's destiny refers, then, to shaping a life that in some way belongs to the individual him- or herself. Doing so is the essence of freedom as I will use that term. If freedom is the ability to follow a course of life that is not already determined, it requires that past and future be connected in a way that does not assure that they will be the same. Then, if the past plays a role in shaping the future, it must be in a way that allows, indeed enables, the future to differ from it.

What makes it possible for the future to differ from the past? To answer this question, Bollas refers us to a concept from Donald Winnicott: the "true self." In a sense, the term "true self" does little more than introduce a term to account for the difference to which I have referred. Observing that people's lives differ one from another in ways that cannot be fully accounted for on the basis of inherited characteristics or cultural imperative, Winnicott introduces a term to refer to an aspect of that inheritance that has the potential to foster the kind of difference we associate with uniqueness and the degree of separation from the past implied in it. This aspect of our inheritance makes the difference associated with uniqueness a link to the past that also creates the possibility that the future will differ from it.

Neither Winnicott nor Bollas considers the emergence of uniqueness in the individual inevitable (Winnicott, 1965). Rather, it depends on the environment in which the human mind finds itself, specifically whether that environment nurtures expressions of the true self or rejects them. This environment transmits the past in the form of ways of relating that either recognize expressions of the true self, accepting their reality in what will become the external world of the child's experience, or it refuses to recognize those expressions as a valid part of the child's experience, one that can play an important role in the emerging trajectory of the child's life.

While I have so far described this process in a language that emphasizes the positive side of the translation of true self into a concrete, particular, life experience, the negative side may, in the end, be more important. What I have in mind by the negative side is that the parent relates to in the child as (potentially) the capacity to negate any way of being already known. When the parent does not already know the child, the child is free not to already know him- or herself. Where this is possible, the parent's relationship with the child enables the child to mobilize the capacity to negate any prior determination or prior knowledge of who he or she is. Indeed, it requires that the child do so. By accepting the negation of what already exists—the past—the parent makes the emergence of uniqueness and of a different future possible.

It is important that, if the child is to live a unique life in "reality," as Bollas insists he or she desires to do, living that life cannot conflict with the negation of reality. This is only possible if reality is configured in a special way: as systems of relating that incorporate the idea of the absence of predetermination. The reality that can be destroyed is the reality the economist Josef Schumpeter (1950) refers to as "creative destruction." The reality of creative destruction places a special burden on the individual who lives in it, and on the child who would develop the capacity to do so. The reality of creative destruction must embody freedom from prior determination as its animating principle. In doing so, it takes something away from the child—security in knowing—so the child can pursue a self-made life.

When we link the experience Winnicott refers to as the "true self" to negating or refusing, we make the essential element in relating the capacity to withdraw from it. This idea of negating the world permeates Winnicott's thinking on early childhood development (Winnicott, 1958, 1962). The capacity to negate, or "negative capability" to borrow a term from John Keats, may depend on inherited characteristics of the individual, but it is not itself inherited. Rather, it is acquired with the development of a rich and complex inner world of a particular kind. Put another way, it is the capacity of the individual to turn inward or dwell in the mind, and therefore negate the outside world, that makes it possible to discover and invent a life uniquely suited to it. By depriving the child of external determination, the parent makes it possible for the child to develop the needed internal resources; indeed, doing so requires that the child develop the needed resources. In this sense, freedom is a capability gained through a specific developmental process.

Choice

The term freedom refers to the presence in our lives of important situations in which what we do is not predetermined for us. Predetermination can operate at different levels. Typically, predetermination refers to the work of external factors that dictate what we do. But the term can also refer to internal factors. Internally, there are two kinds of factors that can pre-determine our conduct for us. The first arise out of our natural condition, or the biological constitution of the human organism.

The second arise from psychological inhibitions on acting that make us feel that what we do is out of our control, that we have no choice but to act and to do so in a particular way.

There are also external factors that restrict our freedom arising out of our existence in a cultural or social context where conduct is dictated by rules and norms, or where what we do is governed by the will of others. This can also be a matter of degree so that freedom exists if there is a significant sphere of living where social rules and the will of others do not fully determine what we do. This sphere is defined most notably by rights. Rights exist to protect the individual from external determination. The more significant and widespread the sphere of rights, the greater our freedom.

Freud focuses attention on freedom as liberation from external constraints in the form of social norms. Indeed, he considers society a necessary, but also emotionally damaging, constraint on freedom, which he speaks about in the language of "liberty," specifically the liberty to pursue the "program of the pleasure principle" (1930a, p. 23). Speaking this way creates an obvious problem Freud himself notes, which is that freedom may only exist outside of society, but it cannot be "defended" there. This means that freedom has no place to call its own. And, yet, the term remains both a powerful element in psychic life, for example as an aspiration, and a significant influence on social institutions, which are constantly under pressure to extend the sphere of rights and therefore of freedom from external determination. Is this preoccupation with freedom simply an illusion, perhaps a defense against awareness of a damaging truth about our situation of the kind to which Freud attempts to draw our attention?

In psychoanalysis, emphasis on internal impediments to freedom in the form of natural imperatives, or drives, and on the power of unconscious processes tends to counter any movement to incorporate a notion of freedom especially as that involves decision making and choice. The latter require that we move beyond the idea of an organism "driven" to do what it does by following the dictates of a force not only held in common by all members of the species but driving all members to act in the same way under similar circumstances, that is to say without expressing anything of importance that is distinctive to the individual unit's response.

Given its intense emotional reality and the important place it occupies in human aspirations, it would be difficult, however, to reduce freedom to nothing more than illusion as Freud's method sometimes tends to do. Thus, even in psychoanalysis, freedom is not necessarily excluded. In this connection, consider the following from Heinz Kohut concerning his struggle with the problem of choice in relation to psychoanalysis. He notes first that, when he began, he was "fully committed to the traditional acceptance of the fact that the domain where the authority of absolute determinism holds sway was unlimited" so that he "could find no place for the psychological activities that go by the name of choice, decision, and free will" (1977, p. 244). Yet, he was already aware that the latter phenomena were "observable through introspection and empathy," and were therefore "legitimate inhabitants of the psychological aspects of reality and the domain of the depth psychologist" (p. 244).

Kohut goes on to identify the domain of psychological phenomena for which the strict determinism associated with the "laws of classical physics" do not apply. He does so by observing that what is required "for their explanation" is the "positing of a psychic configuration—the self—that, whatever the history of its formation, has become a center of initiative: a unit that tries to follow its own course" (pp. 244–245). For our purposes, the significance of Kohut's formulation is that it identifies choice with a psychological configuration: the self. We know that choices are made because there is an active choosing agent present and because a decision has been made that takes us outside the confines of a predetermined program. We cannot know what the decision will be ahead of time or the path chosen by the agent who makes it.

The reality of freedom and choice to which Kohut draws our attention is an *emotional* reality. This is the starting point for any consideration of internal or inner freedom: taking the emotional reality of choice seriously. That emotional reality may be one of struggle and anxiety, of the experience of choice as a burden. Or, it may be the emotional reality of hope and opportunity. In either case, it is no less real and important than the reality of choice in the external world. Indeed, it is the emotional resonance of freedom that sustains and fuels the struggle for freedom and choice in the world outside.

Kohut's comments are based on his observation that the people he works with find themselves in situations where what they do is not programmed for them, in other words where they must choose. Indeed, we might even say that they are beset by choices and the emotionally demanding work of deciding what to do because what they do is not already known to them and there is no authority to which they can appeal capable of relieving them of the burden or opportunity of choosing. This experience is real enough emotionally however, in the end, we judge the internal factors that ultimately determine choice.

To be sure, the internal situation only arises in the absence of external determination of conduct. That is, it only arises where a reasonably robust sphere of individual rights is protected for the individual. But, part of the reason such a sphere exists is the internally originating aspiration to be an agent who makes choices that matter, however emotionally difficult that may be. The starting point, then, is the presence of a powerful aspiration to find ourselves in situations where we must decide what we will do. In response to this aspiration, we place pressure on social institutions to arrange themselves in ways that define a sphere of freedom that did not exist in the state of nature to which Freud alludes when he speaks of the liberty to pursue the program of the pleasure principle. The peculiar liberty of the state of nature is the liberty to live where there is no sphere of self-determination because all that we do is dictated by instinct or drive.

In democratic societies, the pressure placed on social institutions to evolve in ways that enhance freedom expresses the presence in citizens of the conviction that their circumstances can be changed in response to *will*, in this case the will of the majority. This conviction transfers the inner experience of choice into the external world of groups, social movements, and institutions. The idea that the individual can make choices is also the idea that the individual can make changes in his or her circumstances so far as choice is understood in a particular way. Thus, freedom and willful change come to represent two aspects of one reality. Whether the idea of willful change is an accurate translation of freedom and choice into the external world depends on how we understand choice, decision making, and freedom especially as internal realities.

For Kohut, the emotional reality of freedom and choice is the reality of the self, and of conduct determined by the self, or *self*-determined. But all that speaking of the self appears to do is give a name to the internal experience of freedom. It would seem to follow from Kohut's brief comments that we know that an agent is present because choices are made, but it is also the case that we know that choices are made because they originate internally as the expression of the presence of the self. But how do we know that choices are made except that we have posited that there is an agent present who is not programmed to act in the way it acts?

Choosing and thinking

There are choices to be made when individuals can act in different ways and what they do is neither already determined nor externally imposed. This does not mean there are no forces operating on the individual that will affect his or her decision. Choice need not be "free" if by that we mean wholly indeterminate. Choice does mean, however, that the forces operating on the individual are not irresistible. They can be resisted when the individual has the capacity either to act contrary to them or not to act. Choice does not exist where there is one overwhelming impulse, whether that originates internally or externally; nor does it exist when the individual does not have the option of not acting. When we experience ourselves as making a choice, we experience the presence of a margin of indeterminacy with respect to acting. This margin may be no more than a period during which action is suspended. During this period, the action is yet to be determined. That the action is yet to be determined does not mean that no reasons guiding action will emerge during the period of indeterminacy. Where choices are being made, reasons can still play a role. Indeed, it is only where choices can be made that reason has a role to play.

In the absence of a margin of indeterminacy, we may have available a set of options among which we can choose and yet feel we have no choice. In that case, we are not "free to choose," even though it might appear that we are. The feeling that we did not choose even when the outcome was not imposed by external factors is important for understanding why the opportunity and ability to choose matter to the individual. It has often been argued, especially by economists, that the opportunity to choose is essential to assure well-being, in other words that we are significantly better off when choices are available to us. But the issue is considerably more complex than economists tend to assume that it is. While economists emphasize individual preferences and the possibility of acquiring goods that better fit the individual's preferences if he or she is free to choose, what is really central to the matter of choice is what I refer to above as the margin of indeterminacy. To focus our thinking, consider the following example.

> Samuel was a mid-career psychotherapist working with children. He was successful in his profession and felt that it suited him well. Nonetheless, during dinner with college friends, Samuel commented that he felt uncertain about his career because of the way he ended up in it. After college, Samuel did not know what to do next. He did not find himself pointed toward any particular career so, to support himself, he took a job in a day-care center. Presumably, there was something about the work that drew him to it, but he did not at the time consider it a first step toward a career. After working in the day-care center for a year or two, Samuel's supervisor and coworkers encouraged him to pursue a career working with children. They told him that they thought he would be good at the job and that it seemed to suit him. So, Samuel went back to school, got a degree in psychology, and began what became his career.
>
> To all appearances, the outcome was a good one for him. Yet, he felt that, in some sense, he did not really own it because he had never really considered any options. He never really decided on it, but followed a series of steps that, more or less inevitably, led him to it. It seemed from his description that he never really thought much about it. Rather, he followed the advice of his coworkers and, to a significant degree, allowed them to direct him into what became his career. As a result, he felt that he had missed out on something important in his life, which left him feeling dissatisfied.
>
> In response to Samuel's account of his experience, one of his dinner partners quickly disputed his uncertain feelings about his career by reminding him that he was good at what he was doing, that he enjoyed it, and that he was successful. Samuel made it clear in his response that his friend's comment missed the point.

A possible interpretation of Samuel's experience as he reported it would center on the difficult stage of life at which he found himself when he had entered the path to his career (see Erikson, 1959, Chapter 3). At that pivotal moment, he did not know what to do. It would not be unreasonable to wonder if this might also mean that he was unsure about himself, uncertain that there was any career for which he was well-suited, worried about where he might end up if there was no career that fit him well. There is, after all, no reason to be confident of success being an adult in an adult world when you have yet to prove to yourself and others that you possess the necessary capabilities. Samuel's coworkers solved this problem for him by telling him he would be good at this kind of work and encouraging him into it. In so doing, they helped him overcome any self-doubt he might have had. To the extent that his "chosen" career was, in this respect, a solution to the problem of self-doubt, it is not surprising that he felt that there was something faulty in his path to his present situation.

In deciding on his profession, Samuel clearly had a choice if by that we mean faced options none of which would be imposed on him. But, in another sense, he failed to choose since the option he decided on was at least in part chosen to avoid having to choose. He did not undertake a deliberative process. He did not mentally test a variety of alternatives against a reasonably secure knowledge of himself, of who he was and what sort of life would best suit him. To the extent that he did not deliberate, take time to decide, think about himself and the careers he might undertake, he did not choose his career. As a result, twenty years later he felt dissatisfied because, in some sense, he had taken the path of least resistance. When his friend at dinner sought to reassure him, what he actually did was reinforce his uncertainty by repeating the experience he had with coworkers, who, twenty years earlier had sought to help him through his uncertainty by helping him manage his anxiety about his career. Following their advice obviated the need to confront his doubts about himself and to overcome the impulse to allow those doubts to drive him into a preemptive decision whose purpose was, at least in part, to dispel his anxiety.

Samuel's experience highlights the link between choosing and thinking. To make a choice, we must suspend the urge to act and take time to deliberate about our options and how they relate to who we are and what course would best realize our interests and talents. Clearly, if we are to be able to choose, there must be options available to us. But, just as clearly, for us to be able to choose, we must be able to think about our options; we must pause before we act and hold the options in our minds, even seek out new options, without immediately doing anything. To hold them in the mind, we must be able to tolerate the anxiety attached to the uncertainty about the outcome, which in Samuel's case was also uncertainty about himself.

Beyond holding options in the mind, it might, for some choices, be possible to try them out, at least in a preliminary way. If we can try out our options without committing to them, the trial then becomes part of the thought process, adding important information we can use to make a decision. If we add this element, the complexity of choosing becomes even clearer, as does the difference between making choices and impulse-driven conduct.

Choosing involves testing options against our sense of who we are. The idea of finding an option "well-suited" to us suggests a process that involves coming to know who we are, what fits us, and what does not. It involves thought experiments that anticipate what our lives will be like should we choose each of the alternatives. This is true for consequential choices such as the one faced by Samuel, but also for important, but less consequential choices: to live in a house or an apartment, to live in the city, the country, or the suburbs, to add solar panels to our house and drive a hybrid car. It is also true of more mundane choices such as where to go to dinner. In each case, there is a testing process in which we imagine ourselves under the different circumstances resulting from the different choices. This is the sense in which central to choosing is the self taking concrete form as a way of life. To ask, does this option fit who we are is to ask, is it consistent with our central core of being or self.

Contingency

While people sometimes feel that their lives are, as Bollas suggests, the realization or unfolding of their destiny—something preordained for them yet only accomplished by their actions—this feeling can have less to do with the expression of their unique presence and original vitality and more to do with an underlying ambivalence about their power to influence the circumstances in which they find themselves and invest significance in their lives. Linking unique presence to destiny can suggest that uniqueness has been confused with the idea of having a special power to affect the movement of human affairs writ large. The fantasy of having such a power substitutes for the missing conviction that who we are and what we do has any significance in itself. Where this substitution develops, the ability to negate external determination and turn inward has been replaced with the fantasized idea of the ability to create the world. In the absence of an inner world in which the value of the self is well established, there is the over-investment in the external world to which Otto Kernberg draws our attention (1986, p. 246).

If our goal is to understand how the individual integrates a life experience, we may do better if we accept the importance of contingency, an importance that the notion of destiny tends to dismiss. It is not destiny alone that matters, but also what we do with contingency. Turning toward destiny tends to turn contingency into something inevitable when it is not. Rather than inevitability, the use of contingency can invest in it a larger significance by integrating a life experience that is itself contingent. Choice, then, is the active involvement in our lives that integrates contingent events into a more or less coherent whole. The capacity to integrate experience without denying contingency makes life meaningful on a personal level.

To be able to make choices in this sense, we need to call on experiences early in life we did not choose: who our parents happen to be, where we lived, what schools we attended, and who we met there. In a paradoxical way, these experiences, because they were not chosen, are a part of our contingent endowment. The further we are along our development path, the greater our internal resources to call on in making decisions, the better developed our capacity for choice and therefore investing personal meaning in experiences that have none outside the fact that we can make them our own by choosing to have them. Internalization of contingent events and experiences, then, creates the capacity to make choices. This, in turn, lessens contingency and increases the importance of decision making organized around an established and known sense of self.

For Samuel, the more becoming a psychotherapist was experienced as the result of contingent circumstances, and the less it was chosen, the less it could be an expression of an internal factor. For it to be felt as something involving more than contingency, he would have had to choose it, which means he would have had to consider rejecting or negating the possibility that came his way more or less by accident. To be sure, it may be that Samuel chose to work in a day-care center because it was consistent with his emerging identity even if he was not consciously aware of the fact. But, this fact would not, in itself, make his career an expression of his capacity to choose. Instead, it could make it a continuation of an experience of being carried along by events and internal urges born of adaptation to the contingencies of his early life experiences. Samuel had recently graduated from college and his ambivalence about his career could indicate that the emotional work meant to have been completed, specifically the work of forming an internal world well-adapted to choosing, was still unfinished.

Samuel did not feel he had quite reached the point where choosing replaced contingency and he could use contingent circumstances that came his way for his own ends because those ends were well defined. Instead, he remained uncertain about his involvement in finding direction. To use contingency, we must shape the ends/ideas that will integrate our lives. When this happens, we may feel in retrospect that we were destined to do what we did, that contingency was the form of inevitability.

Thinking in this way can integrate our life experience. By seeking inevitability we can find/invest meaning in our lives. In this sense, we choose destiny over fate because otherwise our selves are diminished, our agency eclipsed, we go from the determining power in our lives to being pawns governed in their movement by a power outside. The idea of destiny is an uncomfortable effort to avoid that feeling while at the same time retaining it. When we are destined for great things, those great things are things we do at our own initiative, but they are still great things meant to accomplish great ends that transcend our lives. They express the presence in us of the power to shape *the* world, and not just *our* world.

If there is no contingency, there is no choice, and if there is no choice there is no freedom. Similarly, if life itself depends on our making the right choice, all contingency is contingency of judgment. Only when contingency is about making not the right choice but the one that suits us, that fits the idea we have of ourselves, can there be real freedom. This means that freedom finds its essence in small matters, or more precisely matters that are only large measured against their significance for self-experience.

Choosing and wanting

Beyond its engagement with self-knowledge, choosing also engages another important emotional capacity: the capacity to make what we do matter to us. Samuel's troubled account of the way he arrived in his profession could also mean that he had no strong motivation to have a career. To the degree that Samuel was inhibited in choosing a career path because of his ambivalence about the idea of having a career, his path to his career expressed an impaired capacity to make an emotional investment in a professional life. To make choices, it is not enough that we have options available, or can deliberate about them, we must also care about the outcome. In saying this, I do not mean to suggest that Samuel did not care about his life's work. Rather, I mean to suggest that there remained at some level the sense that succeeding in his career would not provide the gratification he wished for, it would not do for him what, in the depths of his psyche, he wished it would.

What we choose is what we want. To choose, we must know what we want. To know what we want, we must go through a process of finding out, which is the process just outlined for testing possibilities by imagining ourselves realizing them and, in some cases, experimenting with them. The importance of this process tells us something about what we want. The specific emotions that made Samuel's connection to his profession an ambivalent one express failures in the process of coming to know what he wants, a failure to enter into that process in a way that would assure that he would find satisfaction in its outcome.

The failure of this process is a failure in wanting as well as in choosing. Samuel could not be fully satisfied because he had not undergone a process of *making* the object he acquired—his profession—what he wants. It was not just that he had not found what he wanted. Not knowing—coming to know—what he wants, he cannot be satisfied with what he gets.

The process that I have just described for choosing or deciding is synonymous with inner freedom. Another way of formulating the idea is to say that inner freedom is not simply a process for determining what we want, it *is* what we want. While we might be tempted to consider choosing a response to the way the external world is configured and the development of the capacity to choose also a response to external imperatives, in other words a way of adapting to exigencies outside our control, this interpretation is not inevitable. In principle it is as reasonable to say that the world outside is configured as it is so that we will be able to exercise our capacity to make choices, to live a life not predetermined for us. If that is the case, then the world is configured as it is so that we can exercise our capacity to choose as an end in itself.

Freedom and well-being

While economists may offer guidance in the design of institutions that create opportunities for individuals to choose, they tell us little about how individuals gain the capacity to do so and to assure that their choices enhance their welfare. The pursuit of well-being is not simply facilitated by freedom from external constraints. Rather, it requires a significant degree of freedom from the prejudgment or predetermination of what we think and what we do. Understood in this way, well-being is not an already defined state to be pursued, but something yet to be determined. And, it is yet to be determined not *for* us but *by* us, not externally but internally.

For individuals to pursue well-being understood in this way, they must, then, start with the suspension of what is already known about it, especially what the individual already knows about it based on judgments made for him rather than by him. It needs to be emphasized that doing so is no simple or easy task. Suspension of the already known is not something one simply decides to do. What, then, makes it possible for the individual to operate in this way? It turns out that the matter hinges on the ability of the individual to free him- or herself from internal constraints on freedom of movement that parallel those sometimes encountered in the world outside.

To answer our question, then, we need to consider the shape of the individual's internal object world, which depends on the process of internalizing early relationships. Internalization creates a model of relating, or template in the mind, that can then be imposed on subsequent efforts to relate and to use relating in the pursuit of well-being. These subsequent efforts seek to make relating with potential new objects fit the pattern of the internalized connection with an already known object. Suspension of the already known may or may not be an element of the internalized object world formed in this way. If it is not, then suspension of the already known requires a significant change in the configuration of the internal object world.

Whether suspension of the already known is an element of the inner world depends on whether parents relate to their child as yet to be determined and therefore not yet known. When they do, the child can internalize empathic objects and with them a capacity for empathy and for learning about objects, an openness to relating without presuppositions. When, however, the objects provided by parents are not suitable to this end, the capacity for well-being in the sense of the term used here will be seriously impaired, and significant intrapsychic change will be needed if freedom is to be an important part of living for the child.

In psychoanalysis, there are different theories regarding what brings about intrapsychic change that might enable the individual to move outside of the way of relating organized around repetition and adaptation. Among these, one applies especially well to our problem. This is the idea that change occurs because the individual internalizes a new relationship (Fairbairn, 1958). This relationship is new in two ways. First, it differs from the models of relating already in the individual's mind, models that took shape in the effort to manage past relationships. Second, it differs because it involves a new kind of object. The new kind of object has only one quality: listening and the thoughtful effort to understand, in other words, empathy. In a sense, this new object has no distinctive qualities of its own. In Wilfred Bion's formulation (1967), it has neither memory nor desire. It does not impose its own template for relating or act on expectations built into that template. Internalization of the new relationship is the development of a capacity to relate to self and other without already knowing them, which is to say by entering into a process of getting to know them.

To introduce a language I will use here: There is a way of knowing objects in the world that treats them *as if* they were the same as already known objects. And, there is a way of knowing objects that treats them as yet to be discovered. This distinction applies not only to objects in the world outside, but also to that all-important internal object: the self.

Treating potentially new objects as if they are nothing new expresses the dominance in the inner world of object relations that can only be used in a way that assures nothing new will ever be found in the world outside. The starting point for our well-being understood in this way is not the process of satisfying already known needs, but the process of discovering what we need. We can even go so far as to say that well-being means having the capacity and opportunity to find out what we need; and it means finding gratification in that process.

It could, of course, be argued that this is only one notion of well-being, and that there are others. What needs to be emphasized is that this is not a matter of competing notions of well-being and choosing among them or determining which is "right." Rather, it is a matter of different answers to the question: Well-being of what? In a strictly Freudian discussion, this question is answered with reference to the individual defined as a unit of a species and governed by the imperatives built into the natural life of the members of that species. The drive model requires that we consider the matter from this angle. There are also answers to our question that consider the individual a member of a group and well-being as the successful embedding of the individual in the group. By contrast the well-being considered here is the well-being of the self as Kohut speaks of it. What defines the well-being of the self is the degree to which the life within which the self takes on a concrete form of existence is or is not predetermined for it.

If we take this proposition as our starting point, the economist's way of thinking only applies to a limited degree. This is because the economist's method depends on the assumption that what is needed to assure well-being is already known to those whose well-being is at stake in the decisions they make. But one aspect of the economist's method still has relevance. That the individual does not already know who he is and what he wants in his life does not mean that someone else does. This might lead us to accept one part of the economist's method—the idea that the individual is or should be the authority over what he or she needs, while rejecting the other—that the individual already knows what he or she needs. As I hope to show, we can proceed in this way if we define well-being as that state of mind marked by the presence there of an empathic object and as the activity emanating out of that state of mind. This state of mind is the one Winnicott (1986) refers to as being "in contact with the self," and the activity emanating out of it as the "doing that expresses being."

Freedom of thought

Being in contact with the self is closely linked to what I will refer to as freedom of thought or the free movement of thoughts and of the ideas that organize them. What blocks free movement of thoughts is the fear of what we will find out about ourselves if we allow our thoughts to be fully available to us. When freedom of thought is associated with having painful thoughts and becoming aware of deeply entrenched and painful ideas we have about ourselves, we develop strategies designed to block the thoughts and the ideas they represent. This situation should be central to any discussion of well-being. We cannot live well if our life mainly consists of the struggle to block thoughts from occurring to us, and, if that is not possible, to disconnect those thoughts from ideas about us for which those thoughts act as signals. Following a predetermined program built around rigid defenses blocks the development of internal freedom as the free flow of thoughts and the movement of ideas. Winnicott speaks of this in terms of the flexibility and rigidity of defenses and suggests that "... it is the rigidity of the defence organisation that makes people complain of the lack of freedom" (1986, p. 231).

There are thoughts and ideas that must not be brought to mind, but instead remain immobilized or fixed as the process of idea formation that involves working on our thoughts and our ideas about them cannot be engaged lest it reveal the unthinkable thoughts and the self-destroying idea. Strategies that prevent the free movement of thoughts and ideas include the effort to provoke programmed responses in self and others and to make relating consist of responses of this kind. When this program includes provocation of aggression against the self, identification with the aggressor then makes the external attack internal and provokes the use of defenses against escape from identification with the internal victimized self. The demand for freedom from oppression now also expresses the presence of powerful defenses against inner freedom.

Winnicott also suggests that inner freedom "cannot easily be destroyed" (p. 232). This is because the internal situation we associate with inner freedom reflects the strength of internalized good object relations and can only be lost where the internal objects that support it are displaced by an identification with bad objects. Just as the formation of good internal objects results from a sustained experience relating to good objects in the outside world, their displacement also depends not on momentary exposure to bad objects or their intent to do harm, but sustained exposure under circumstances that weaken defenses against them.

The free movement of thoughts only becomes freedom if the movement of thoughts can set us free. But, in itself, it cannot. Free association, daydreaming, and reverie only free us so far as they lead to or provide the material for a process that alters our emotional connection to ideas that integrate our thoughts in ways we associate with unfreedom. Freedom of the inner world is an interpretation of our thoughts that (1) allows us to have them, (2) enables us to understand what they mean in a way that frees us from self-destructive interpretations.

This notion of freedom of the inner world can be connected to freedom in the world outside, or freedom in our relations with others. An obvious place to start, and one clearly running parallel to internal freedom, is the freedom we associate with living in a private space, a space within which we exert our dominion, a space where relating to others is regulated by us and not for us. Privacy as a right, for example in the form of private property, represents, in the world outside, the safety and comfort of the self in the inner world. Our private space in the world outside mirrors the availability to us of private internal space. On one side, our ability to tolerate privacy as an external matter, for example by being alone, expresses the comfort we experience in being in our inner world since privacy as an external matter is experienced as safety in the inner world. On the other side, we can only experience inner freedom when we can (have the right to) exclude others from interacting with us, or when our interactions with them are not made contingent on giving up being with ourselves (Levine, 2017).

As long as our thoughts stand outside any interpretative process, the reason we have those thoughts will remain opaque. We experience our thoughts as having no reason to be: They are what they are. Typically, this is the way we experience our emotions, and therefore the interpretation of ourselves and our situation embedded in them. We are either driven by reason or by emotion, and the only way to be guided by reason is to repress emotion. This judgment is, however, the opposite of the truth because emotions are interpretations of the world and are, therefore, a primitive form of reason.

We can retrieve the opposition, however, in an altered form: Emotions are interpretations that act as givens because the reasons for them are hidden from us. Indeed, the emotion is all about hiding reasons so that thinking—reason—can be superseded by acting. To break the immediacy of the connection between emotion and acting, we have to contain rather than repress our emotions, to understand their meaning through a thinking process, and transform them into a consciously held interpretation. Thus, emotions are both rational and irrational; they can be the enemy of reason or its starting point.

We can see, then, what it means for psychoanalysis to reveal the reason in the seemingly irrational. Doing so also means that psychoanalysis sees reason not simply when results are caused by consciously intended action and can therefore be attributed to a causal subject, but also when this is not the case and reasons are implicit or embedded. Seemingly irrational conduct is conduct for which the reasons are not apparent even to the actor herself, including conduct that seems irrational when set against the standard of achieving consistently held and reality-connected ends. On one level, the psychoanalytic process is the process of searching for embedded reasons. Embedded reasons are also reasons that drive conduct without operating through conscious intent.

Freedom to relate

Roger Kennedy, in his book on the "freedom to relate," speaks of the freedom "to experience one's own transference with all of the detail of how one sees oneself and others." Awareness of the transference has a broad significance as "the distillation of [individuals'] whole way of relating, including the way they picture the world and talk about it and other people" (1993, p. 73). While Kennedy tends to separate this freedom from self-interest and to give relating the central place, if we include in self-interest an in-depth awareness of the self and a significant experience of its presence, and, if we take into account that relating has nothing free about it where the self is absent, then one is free to relate only insofar as one is present in relating. Being present is another way of speaking about having "the experience of the transference," although it may be more precise to say knowing rather than having that experience—having in the sense of *owning*, rather than having as opposed to knowing.

Only if we become aware (conscious) of the meaning of our self-state and of the way others are incorporated into it can we decide not to act within the template set by pre-existing internalized object relations. Only then can we free ourselves from ways of relating we are otherwise driven to reproduce by forces both unknown and familiar. This is a richer meaning of choice than the one favored in economics, where choosing simply means deciding among more than one option where no external constraint dictates the outcome. In the alternative view, choosing means that what we do and how we relate are free of determination by internal imperatives over which we have no control because we are unaware that they exist and shape the meaning of what we do and how we relate. Doing and relating are always driven by the meaning invested in situations. But only when their real or true meaning is known to us is freedom of choice a possibility.

When we think about internal imperatives that block a process that makes deliberation among alternatives possible, anxiety is of special importance. Anxiety and elevated levels of aggression linked to it block contact with the self. By contrast, the feeling of safety in being creates the necessary setting for self-directed action. Anxiety makes dwelling in the mind synonymous with emotional suffering. It follows that a necessary condition for well-being understood in the way I have suggested is a feeling of safety as an internal matter.

The danger to the self that makes it feel unsafe may originate outside as an aspect of the experience of relating to others. When it is systematic enough, however, the attempt to defend the self against this external danger can lead to internalization of the relationship in which the self is put at risk. When the threat is internalized, the response to it becomes a permanent state of mind. When this happens, the free movement of thoughts and ideas is no longer possible because the free movement of ideas is now the danger against which we must defend ourselves. It is not surprising, then, that dogmatic insistence on a belief system takes hold and the effort to impose that system on others becomes an important part of a strategy to block the free moment of ideas. When this happens, the possibility of thinking without presuppositions is lost.

There are two kinds of threat: the threat *to* the self and the threat emanating *from* it. There are two levels of safety: safety in the inner world and safety in the world outside. And, there are two kinds of safety: safety through adaptation and safety from adaptation. The individual can pursue safety through alignment with the attack on the self, as in identification with the aggressor. Doing so involves directing aggression toward the self and putting in place a false self based on compliance with a template for relating set externally. The result is adaptation to living an as-if life in an as-if world. Alternatively, the individual can pursue safety through contact with an empathic internal object that makes it possible for what he or she does to express an internal process free of the need to adapt to predetermined ways of being, doing, and relating.

CHAPTER 2

Memory

Bad memories

The kind of freedom to which I have referred can play an important part in linking the subject matter of psychoanalysis—the inner world— to the study of the world outside, where the term freedom is assumed to have its natural home in shaping social institutions. But limiting the term freedom to social institutions limits access to an important way of thinking about psychic life. This limitation is especially unfortunate because the notion of freedom when applied to the inner world suggests an important link between the two spheres of human experience: the internal and the external. Corresponding to these two spheres are two kinds of freedom. Both are possible; but neither is inevitable. They are closely connected. Without external freedom, inner freedom cannot develop. Without internal freedom, external freedom does not matter.

The tendency to equate freedom with external freedom expresses a hope: the hope that all we need to become free is to enter into a sphere of life where no one has the right to determine what we do. The goal embedded in this hope is typically referred to in the language of power and rights: Freedom is freedom from the power of others to determine what we do, which is also the right to determine what we do for our-selves. At the core of this hope is the wish that our unhappiness will be alleviated if we can free ourselves from the power others have over us because it is their exercise of power over us that makes us unhappy. This wish expresses an important connection: the connection between unfreedom and unhappiness.

While external freedom is freedom from the tyranny of others, inter-nal freedom is freedom from the tyranny we exert over ourselves. Tyr-anny in the inner world is not, however, independent of the shape relating to others takes. Rather, tyranny in the inner world develops out of ways of relating with others that instantiate unfreedom. When these ways of relating are internalized, the inner world becomes a place in which we feel assaulted and diminished. But the fact that inner tyranny results to a large degree from internalization of unfreedom in relating does not mean that it can be relieved simply by escaping an external world in which we are not free, or by somehow making the external world a bet-ter place than it is. This is because, once internalized, unfreedom takes on a life of its own as we now become the source of our own oppression. When this happens, freedom from tyranny in the external world cannot relieve us of our unhappiness.

The tyranny of the inner world takes form as the tyranny of unwanted or "bad" memories. We are tormented by these unwanted memories, or "reminiscences" as Freud and Breuer term them. One of the reasons memories are connected to unhappiness is that memories act as a warn-ing system by reminding us of situations in which bad things happened. By recalling the consequences of being in those situations, bad memories motivate us to avoid them in the future, to alter our path if recurrence of the bad event is, or is imagined to be, imminent.

Our memory warning system establishes a primitive template for what, later in life, we speak of as learning from history. Our history, or past experience, provides a useful guide to decision making in the pres-ent so far as the situations we find ourselves in do not differ in what is essential about them from those situations recorded as memories; in other words, so far as the future does not differ from the past. Other-wise, learning from history can come to mean understanding present and future as the recurrence of the past even if they need not be; and this can, in turn, lead us to define all situations according to the template provided by memory. All that we do then falls under the law of repetition. The system designed to warn us against repeating bad experiences drives us to repeat them because it excludes alternatives.

Where bad memories dominate, the emotional state associated with the equation of past, present, and future is the one we refer to in the language of anxiety. Anxiety is the anticipation of the recurrence of damage done to us in the past; it is an aspect of the movement of experience from the external world to the internal. This movement then shapes what we do, which becomes activity whose end is to relieve us of our anxiety by avoiding recurrence of the situation we recall to mind, or, if that is not possible, by rewriting the script for our conduct so the outcome of the situation is not what it once was. Thus, while under the rule of recurrence, the situation in present and future is defined as the same as the situation experienced in the past, our response to it need not be, or we may assume that it need not be. Whether this is true or not depends on the degree to which we are limited in what we do and how we interpret the anticipated situation. In other words, anxiety serves a productive purpose if we have freedom of thought and movement: freedom of thought that allows us to conceive alternate responses to our situation, and freedom of action that allows us to respond differently than we have in the past.

Freedom of thought and movement marks a difference in the organism from what it would be were it programmed to do what it does and to treat all situations as those to which its programming applies, including that programming Freud refers to in the language of the pleasure principle. What differs in the uniquely human experience of the world is freedom from programming. Once this freedom is established, it is possible for anxiety to attach itself to a new aspect of experience as there is now also the experience of freedom itself and of the possibility that we might lose it: in Kohut's language, the freedom of the individual to constitute him or herself as a center of initiative. Our anxiety now centers on the loss of freedom rather than the loss of pleasure, though the latter can still play an important role, especially when pleasure is associated with the exercise of freedom taken as an end in itself.

So far as bad events are bad because in them we experienced a loss of freedom, memories serve to remind us of our unfreedom and its consequences: loss of gratification and diminution of the self. Freedom of the inner world is freedom from these memories. But, freeing ourselves from our memories and the recurrence they attempt to impose on us is no simple matter. This is because not only do our memories act as warning signals, they are also bound up with our sense of who we are: our way of being as that takes shape in a personal identity. For some people, personal identity is little more than the instantiation of a warning system as a way of life and way of thinking. To the extent that this is the case, internal freedom is limited and external freedom of little use.

Our memories contain, or have attached to them, the meaning we invest in the salient experiences of our lives, whether good or bad, and the ways of relating that express or realize that meaning. When memories are attached to emotion, they contain what is meaningful in our existence. To lose our memories is to lose our existence as a center of the special kind of experience we associate with being present. Because of this, we cannot simply purge our memories from our inner worlds. To do so would leave us without any way to know who we are and find our way in the world outside. While our memories may make us unhappy or define us as unhappy selves, to lose them would create an unhappiness of a higher order: the unhappiness associated with the feeling, even conviction, that we do not exist. To avoid this higher-order unhappiness, we must hold onto our memories and the unhappy self they instantiate.

The term unfreedom, when applied to the inner world, refers to a situation there that limits what thoughts we are able to hold in mind and think about. Freedom, that is, refers to a situation in which our thoughts are never taboo. Our thoughts become unthinkable when having them is felt to pose a threat, most notably to our connection with our good objects and by extension our good self. Considered in reverse, having taboo thoughts means connecting to a bad self, one undeserving of connection with a good object. The taboo applied to thoughts deemed bad necessarily applies to memories, which make up a significant proportion of the content of our thought processes. To protect the mind from the danger posed by bad thoughts, those thoughts are blocked from being thought.

The presence of the unacceptable thoughts is felt in the rigidity of adherence to the thoughts that substitute for them, for example the thought that the unacceptable thoughts exist outside, in others. Rigidity marks unfreedom as an internal matter. Only what is already known independently of any thinking process can be brought to mind. To think is to doubt the thought put in place to block the bad thoughts from being thought. All thoughts are predetermined in the sense that they come to mind fully formed rather than emerging out of a process whose outcome is not yet known.

This strategy for coping with thoughts is sometimes spoken about in the language of defenses. We can repress our memories so that, while they still exert a powerful influence over what we do and how we feel, we are not aware of them. Or, we can attempt to provoke others to experience our memories for us. The problem is that the memories remain; it is only our awareness of them that has been limited. This means that the unhappiness associated with our memories remains as well. That unhappiness is now expressed in the strategies used to dismiss our connection to our memories.

Defenses can be considered a form of forgetting. But we cannot resolve the problem memory poses for us simply by forgetting. We do not exert that kind of control over memory, which is too deeply and essentially bound up with our way of being. To free ourselves from our memories without ceasing to exist, we must find a way to come to terms with them. We must locate them and, rather than purging them from our minds, defuse their power over us. Thus, to escape our unhappiness, we must forget; but to forget is to suffer the loss of the record of our presence in our lives.

The dilemma just summarized only arises, of course, when bad memories dominate to the point that we cannot exist in their absence, when we have nothing to call on to diminish their power over us. This means that the logical solution to our problem is to engage in the kinds of relationships that create "good" memories. This might be easily done were it not the case that our memories are what we use to guide us in shaping our relations with others. Because of this, the way we understand relating, which is embedded in memory, drives us not to find good relationships that will, over time, replace the dominance of bad memories, but to reproduce the bad relationships and thereby create additional memories that are not new but are, in their essentials, the same as the old ones. These "new" relationships, far from creating memories that displace the old, only reinforce their power over us.

This reinforcement of memories of past experiences is work linked to an important aspect of our memories and their connection to our sense of who we are: the sense of inevitability attached to the remembered experience as that is transposed into the present. This sense of inevitability underpins the power of the remembered experience to replicate itself in the present, or the "compulsion to repeat." Repetition confirms the inevitability of the bad experience. In the world of repetition, everyone is the same person; and it is this inability to imagine or conceive something different that assures we will never discover anything different. In other words, the compulsion to repeat expresses the presence in the individual of an impairment in the creative capacity in the world of human relations, or, in other words, of the capacity to conceive the possibility of a self that is not already known.

Memories shape conduct when they become implicit theories of relating or represent not simply a record of an event but an idea about the world. When this happens, the record of the event takes on a larger significance. In part this is because the record of an event comes to stand in for a set of like experiences so that, while the memory seems to be about something concrete and particular, it also represents something more general; it is, in Kernberg's words, a coming together of emotionally invested memory "traces" (Kernberg, 1976, p. 29). Not only, however, does this general significance come to be attached to a particular event, but the event also becomes a stimulus to a mental struggle to come to terms with the emotions embedded in other events and attached to the memories of them. As this struggle evolves within the context of the recurrence of the event at different times and under different circumstances, the meaning of the event becomes part of the understanding of self and other.

One important aspect of this evolution is the way the event comes to spawn more or less elaborate narratives involving how we wish we had managed it differently, how we might go about avoiding it in the future, or, in the case of good memories, what we might do to make the event, or events like it, occur again in the future. In other words, the process of remembering gives birth to fantasies, which are, in this respect, aspects of memory. The process of integrating memories into a more general whole leads to the development of internal objects and object relations.

To summarize: Memories involve particular people engaged in specific acts at specific times in specific settings. But they also represent the power behind the repetition of patterns of relating, they are implicit theories or interpretations of relating and of the self as it exists in its connections with others. To disrupt the closed system created through repetition of remembered relationships, what must be introduced to the inner world is not simply another relationship to take its place among the existing artifacts of our past life, but a new interpretation or idea of relating.

The power of the closed system exerts itself through a specific theory of change, which I will refer to as "willful change." At the center of this theory is the idea that there is present in the mind a factor or agency existing outside memory and the interpretations of experience embedded in memory. This factor is capable of separating change from the power of the past as that power is instantiated in memory and identity. Put another way, according to this theory, the self is capable of acting independently of itself.

The power of the idea of willful change represents the presence within the psyche of an idea about freedom expressive of the wish that what we do could be separated from who we are. This is not the freedom to have our memories, which I refer to as the free movement of thoughts, but the freedom to dismiss the power of memory by an act of will. What willful change actually dismisses, however, is not the power of memory, but our awareness of that power. By so doing, far from removing the power of memory, it assures that it will be the controlling factor, since we cannot influence let alone overcome the power of a force the presence of which lies outside our awareness. Real change begins with the awareness of the power of memory; in other words, it begins not with forgetting, but remembering. But, unlike closed system thought processes, it uses memory as a way of undermining its power. It does so by reinterpreting the experience represented in the memory of it. It alters the idea for which memory and the emotion attached to it is the primitive form.

The deficiencies of willful change do not make freedom an illusion. While the freedom of willful change may be illusory, there is another freedom consistent with the formation of the self into a way of life embedded in salient memories and the kinds of relations they foster in the present. For there to be a freedom consistent with the power of memory, there must be a special kind of memory. Put simply, if there are sufficiently powerful memories of relationships shaped by respect for our freedom, the capacity for change can develop as an expression of them. This does not mean that unhappiness will be eliminated, but it does mean that a special kind of unhappiness can be moderated to the point that it does not prevent our being in our lives as an active factor.

Replicants

To further explore the relation of memory to freedom, I will consider a public fantasy in which the matter is central: the two *Blade Runner* films (1982, 2017). Both depict a future that has the appearance of a decayed past. In this respect, the films depict memory: the memory of a lost world frozen in time, indeed a destroyed world, though not a memory of the destruction of the world. This tells us something important about how our past is experienced in the present: as a destroyed future.

In the destroyed-world fantasy of the film *Blade Runner 2049*, there are two kinds of people: real and replicant. The difference between the two is captured in words spoken late in the film: real people are "born not made." To be born is to have a mother, a family, and the kinds of experiences that make family an emotional reality for us. To be made is to come into existence as an adult without the experience of becoming an adult. Thus, in an early scene in the original film, a "blade runner" (policeman who hunts replicants) is testing whether a subject is a replicant. The test consists of a series of questions meant to elicit emotional responses detected in their physical manifestations. The last question he asks is: "Tell me about your mother." The replicant responds by shooting him (*Blade Runner*, 1982). Replicants do not have mothers. What replicants have to represent mothers are photographs of other people's mothers. What real people have is a childhood made up of emotionally important experiences instantiated as memories, and objects such as photographs that recall their memories to mind. Those who are born have "real" memories; those who are made have artificial or implanted memories. Artificial memories are memories of experiences they never had. Real memories are the mental residue of actual events and relationships.

Replicants are nonhuman slaves built to do jobs humans do not want to do. The blade runner's job is to find and kill—"retire"—replicants that have liberated themselves from servitude to humans. Some replicants, especially the most technically advanced, long to be human.

Some imagine that they are. And, for some, the question of their human-ness is unresolved. Because they appear to be human, they can blend into human settlements and live as humans. To prevent them from doing so, the blade runner must seek them out and retire them.

Replicants are not alive but only appear to be. This presence in the world of replicants passing as human, the absence of life passing as life, poses a threat and, for that reason, the replicants who attempt to pass for humans must be hunted down and killed. One way to under-stand the threat posed and the need to purge the world of it is to under-stand the drama of the films as an internal drama and the threat as a threat to the inner world. The greatest danger to emotional life is the prospect that a false self will replace what is real and true in the person-ality; that, over time, all vestiges of the true self will have been replaced by the replicant. Thus, the blade runner's greatest fear is that he or she is a replicant but does not know it.

Real memories are the way we experience the emotional meaning of our past and carry it forward into the present. They are our way of connecting ourselves to the experiences that made us who we are. This is what makes them real. Our memories can be said to be the presence of the self in the mind as a concrete reality formed of particular experi-ences. Without our memories, we cannot secure our sense of continu-ity in being. Indeed, our memories are the continuity of our being and evidence of the presence of the self in our lives. But, if we are unable to integrate our memories into a cohesive whole, then we cannot secure the conviction that we exist as an enduring emotional unit, in other words, as a capacity to invest meaning in what we do and have done in the past. Thus, as Kohut points out, "In the last analysis, only the experience of a firmly cohesive nuclear self will give us the conviction that we will be able to maintain the sense of our enduring identity, however much we might change" (1977, p. 182). Continuity in change is the reality of the self as a personal identity that endures.

By making memories, we make our lives real, but only if we can make our own memories. Our life is not real if our only memories are memories of a life we did not have. The metaphor of the film, then, tells us something important about what we need. As the man who created the replicants tells us, the replicants "needed memories." This statement only reinforces the humanness of replicants, because to need memories is to be human. We need to have in our lives the residue of real experiences formed into the contents of our inner world, in other words, we need a rich experience of ourselves. This residue of real experiences also takes the form of the things we need, own, and surround ourselves with. In other words, we need emotionally meaningful experiences and the objects that provoke our memories of them. We need objects because, and to the extent that, they are resonators of memory.

Replicants have no such experience, therefore no continuity of being, and therefore no internal or self-experience. What appear to them as experiences through which they became who they are were made by others to create in them the illusion of having a childhood and a family. It follows that being made rather than born means coming into existence fully formed on a template or plan made by others. The replicants are "designed" and manufactured. Because they are not made by others, those who are born have the opportunity to make themselves. Most of those in the film were not born and never will be. Toward the end of the original film, one of the blade runners comments about a female replicant: "It's too bad she won't live, but then again who does?" He thus calls into question the existence of humans by calling into question the difference between humans and replicants.

The difference between real people and replicants is a metaphor for a difference between two ways of being that people experience in themselves: being fully determined by others, and participating in a process of self-determination. For the replicants, life is an illusion because memories are an illusion. The replicant represents a kind of person—the kind of person who has no life. The replicant is a person wholly identified with a false self created to hide the truth that, at the core of the replicant's being, there is only empty space. For the replicant, the purpose of memories is to prevent contact with what is real about their lives and themselves because contact with that reality—life without memories—would be intolerable.

There is, however, a contradiction built into this construction. It is only necessary to protect the replicant from his or her reality to the extent that the feelings provoked by life without memories would be intolerable, which is only the case if the replicant has an emotional core, albeit one wholly taken over by a longing to be real, which is to be born not made. But longing to be real is a human experience of the most basic kind and indicates the humanness of the replicant. This means that denial of the humanness of the replicant is also denial of the humanness of the humans who created it. More specifically, it is denial of the human longing to be real and alive, which is denial of our sense that what is real and alive in us has been impaired, if not lost. This makes the replicant the locus of our doubts about the reality of ourselves.

The presence of this longing reinforces our conviction that the replicants in the films represent an aspect of the way humans experience themselves. This way of thinking about it makes the films not narratives of a struggle between two different classes of people, but of a struggle within one kind of person: humans. And, the doubt about humanness that is central to the films is doubt about having been born, and therefore doubt about the reality of our memories.

There is nothing unusual in individuals harboring false memories about their childhoods and especially their relationships with their parents, including doubts that they *had* parents if by that we mean they had adults in their lives able and willing to care about and for them, to nurture them in their process of maturation to adulthood. What they had in their lives instead were adults pretending to be parents, but incapable of occupying that role. This pretense of parenting is what the child comes to remember, and, in this sense, the child's memories are implanted to substitute for, and hide the reality of, the absence of memories of real parents.

The absence of memories as depicted in the films represents the absence of an internalized empathic object capable of providing a safe space in which the child can mature. In this regard, it may be worth noting that, in the novel on which both films were based, the difference between replicants and humans is formulated explicitly in the language of empathy. When you look to a replicant for acknowledgement of your humanness you get none (Dick, 1968). Instead, what you get is a cold feeling provoked by the absence of emotional connection. Understood in this way, what the film depicts in the form of false memories and the photographs that represent them is the absence of an internalized parental relationship of a special kind. Thus, even if, in the physical sense of the term, this child was born, no birth in the emotional sense of the term ever occurred. The adult the child became was made for him by his parents and by the fantasy of the family they implanted as a substitute for the reality of absence.

In the end, the false parent is held responsible for the plight of the replicant, and the struggle for life becomes a struggle against the false parent. This is why, towards the end of the film, life is equated with the struggle against the forces that would keep us from being born or giving birth. Endless longing becomes an endless struggle against oppression. It becomes hate. That it does so tells us something about why it is not possible to have a life. It tells us what caused the destruction of the world: the presence in the world of a figure who wants to make us into a replica rather than encourage us to have a life of our own. When this figure succeeds, the result is a destroyed inner world.

The birth of the self

The second *Blade Runner* film is driven by the idea that there can be, and perhaps already exists, a replicant with the capacity to create life by giving birth. If such a replicant can be found, it will be possible to overcome dependence on those who made replicants for what life the replicants have and replace them with a real mother. The protagonist of the film is a blade runner sent to hunt down and kill the replicant with the power to create life. The tension in the film takes the form of a struggle within the blade runner over whether he will kill this new form of replicant or save her. He has powerful memories about the reality of which he is uncertain. His hunt for the replicant becomes a search for the truth about his memories, which is the truth about himself. He hopes and imagines that the special replicant he has been tasked to find will turn out to be his mother.

The narrative of the film becomes a narrative of the search for the birth mother. The replicant that can create life is a replica that does not replicate but gives birth. But this is a contradiction in terms. Replicants cannot be born because that would require someone to design the capacity to negate their creation, to design the capacity to negate design. It necessitates that those who would design us choose instead to facilitate our process of self-development, in other words be parents rather than engineers. In the film, this contradiction is resolved through the attempt to design a more accurate replica of a human, one that includes the capacity to give birth, without the peculiarly human process of development, which is a process of *self*-development. Thus, it is assumed that, if the design process, which is the enemy of humanness, can be perfected, it will produce humans, made not born, but nonetheless humans. This is the core fantasy of the film and the core hope of the replicant and those in the world the replicant represents: that parental failure was a failure of skill and ingenuity on the part of those who made us replicants ignoring the central problem, which is that they did so *by design*. The problem resulting from creation by design cannot be solved by finding a better design.

Put in the language used here, the problem is how to create inner freedom by design, which is to say without the experience of freedom in relations with others in an intimate setting. Inner freedom depends on internalization of suitable relationships, so the problem is how to establish inner freedom without the experience of those relationships. In the language of the film, this is a question of memory: How do we create memories out of whole cloth that can serve to make the inner world a safe place to be? This is a vital question for those whose growing-up experience was in an unsafe place, those whose parents were inadequate to the job and yet were all they had.

Blade Runner 2049 offers the viewer an external depiction of an internal situation. In the depiction, the different characters in the film represent different characters in the individual's inner world, or different internal objects. Central to this situation is the struggle for freedom on the part of the replicants and the resistance to it on the part of humans. The struggle for freedom, understood as taking place in fantasy, is not a struggle between individuals or groups, but within the individual. This is an endless struggle imagined to create a world in which replicants can be born and make memories. But that is nothing more than a wish: the wish that someone who was made not born can become human by defeating those who made her and thereby overcoming the servitude implied in having been made. But the only world into which she would be born is the destroyed world of a post-apocalyptic dystopia. Everything is dead or dying; everything is a colorless grey; everything is occluded by dust; all are poisoned. This is the world to be won by the struggle against the maker. As it turns out, in this world all there can be is an implanted dream meant to enable the replicant to hold onto a baseless hope.

That this is the case becomes clear if we consider the possible outcomes of the struggle. If the slaves succeed in killing their masters and setting themselves free, then, having freed themselves of the demand to devote their lives to dehumanizing work, who will do the work for them? Will they design new replicants to do their work? On the other side, if the humans succeed in killing all the runaway replicants, they will have killed their only hope for freedom since that hope resides in and is represented by the runaway replicant. When the terms of the dilemma are formulated in this way, as they are in the films, no solution is possible. Indeed, it is this formulation of the internal situation that locks in unfreedom as an internal matter.

Off-world

One scene from *Blade Runner 2049* tells us something important about the internal situation depicted in the film. The scene opens with the blade runner wandering through a dystopian landscape where he encounters a group of children. The children take him to a factory where hundreds of children are at work. Their supervisor tells the blade runner that they are scavengers collecting scrap metal to be used in the production of ships built to take humans to a "grand life off-world." This, he is told, is as close as these children will get to escape from Earth.

Here Earth represents the site of the destroyed world. Taken as a representation of the inner world, the scene suggests that those on Earth—and all the characters in the films are Earth-bound—are doomed to a life of toil in a dystopian world, toil that will make it possible for others to escape. But, in the film, there are no others; no one escapes or has escaped. Indeed, the only escapees are the replicants who sought freedom not in living off-world where they were slaves, but in returning to Earth where they were made.

The child-labor scene represents one version of the inner child as it exists in the world of *Blade Runner*. But there is another: the child born of the union of replicant and blade runner (who may or may not be a replicant) from the first film. By the time of the second film, this child has grown to be a young adult. Originally, she was meant to escape Earth for an off-world colony, but an autoimmune deficiency prevented her from travel and forced her to live in a sealed-off chamber where she has become uniquely skilled in designing memories for replicants, memories in which the replicants had a happy family life in a bucolic setting. Because these memories are not real, while they are experienced as memories, they are better understood as fantasies intended to soften the otherwise harsh and perhaps intolerable life of the replicants. When our family life is experienced emotionally as a life of child labor, it only becomes tolerable if those for whom we labor implant in us happy images of a false childhood. Indeed, it is possible to interpret the distinction in the film between real and false memories as the difference between memory and fantasy.

You cannot live with humans unless you can protect yourself from the virus that has infected them. If your immune system is defective, then you must isolate yourself from others. A defective immune system is the same thing as being receptive to emotional communication. Emotional connection with others allows them to communicate their feelings about their damaged selves to us, threatening our own contact with ourselves. This is the virus that takes the form of false memories. To protect ourselves from this virus we seal our true selves off from any emotional contact with others. In the inner world, there is a favored child sealed away in a dream world, a child for whom contact with others is life-threatening. Locked away in isolation, she creates beautiful dreams of a world (the "off-world") that can only exist in imagination. Her role in the drama of the inner world that is the film is to create the false memories that make living there tolerable, if only barely so.

Also, in the inner world there are the less-favored children who have no special talent. They are the ones who are unable to make beautiful dreams of a world and because of that find themselves living the dystopia of inner space. The talent they lack is essentially the talent to create and believe in fantasy. These two kinds of children are the internal representations of two radically conflicting aspects of the individual's childhood, both of which involve imprisonment: one to protect a creative but fragile self, the second to engage in self-destroying work so others (their makers) can travel off-world and thus escape the life-deadening world of the family. But there are no others, and the off-world of the dream does not exist.

The films explore a common fantasy solution to the problem of the loss of inner freedom. The fantasy solution follows from an understanding of how inner freedom was lost. It was lost when parenting was taken over by a scientist-engineer and the good object was replaced by an object intent on programming the child for a predetermined life rather than nurturing a process whose outcome is yet to be determined. Loss of inner freedom results when the parenting process becomes a process of shaping the child according to an externally given model with the resulting loss of contact with the self and the secure knowledge of what is real about it. That knowledge is lost when self-determination is replaced by replication.

Continuity of being

The replicant is programmed to do what it does. To the extent that the replicant exhibits an incipient humanness, it can only be discerned in actions that cannot be attributed to its programming, those human moments when the replicant defies its designer's purpose and acts for itself. So far, however, as the replicant operates within the limits of its design, it cannot make choices. This inability to make choices is closely linked to the matter of implanted memories, and to the quality of memories that make them real. What we are told about this difference is that real memories are not distinguished by being more vivid, but by being "messy," where messy refers to their involvement with emotion.

Real memories are involved with emotion in a special way. Not only are emotions attached to the memory so that to call the past experience to mind is to activate the emotion attached to it, but the experience of the emotion is inextricably linked to the memory that activates it, so that the experience of the emotion *is* the activation of the memory. The memory represents the emotions originally felt in the experience internalized as a memory. An emotion becomes important when it is repeated in an important relationship so that the memory of that relationship is inseparable from the internal presence of the salient emotion or emotional configuration.

The internalized relationship represented in memories contains the meaning we had for others and, through internalization, we now have for ourselves. Thus, a single event in an ongoing relationship comes to represent the relationship and the many events that made up that relationship. Those events are not all "remembered" individually but are all recalled in a single memory. This representative memory does important emotional work, and the form it takes results from the internalization process made consistent with that work. In other words, what is called to mind is not memory understood as a photographic record of an event, but memory as the narrative form of a way of understanding a relationship by mentally appropriating it as an emotional configuration, in other words as an internal object.

Because memory instantiates the meaning of relating, it is essential to the continuity of being the replicants sought to find in the tangible evidence (e.g. photographs) of their implanted memories but could not find there. This continuity of being is essential for choice because it is the concrete form taken by the presence of the self as the seat of agency. Choice refers not to an inexplicable whim but to the expression of the self and the use of the self in the effort to come to a decision, which is a decision about what course of action best fits the self and expresses its unique presence, a unique presence that can be found in the memories understood in the way just suggested. The choice is then made according to its link to being or existing in and through an integrated series of choices. Without real memories there is no continuity of being and therefore no way to make choices. And, without the self, there is no integrated series of choices. There is only recourse to programmed response. Choices express in what we do the personality built up out of the internalization of relationships represented in those salient memories whose connection to emotion indicates their meaning.

Willful change

If the term "self" refers to the force within the personality that integrates memories and the internalized relationships they represent, then the self only exists in and through those memories. We have seen this in the dilemma of the replicant, who has no real memories and therefore does not exist. The self does not exist outside of memory, selecting which events in life to hold onto and which to let go of; rather, the self exists as the memory system. Or, more precisely, the self exists in and through the effort to hold onto memories and the emotional experiences they represent. But this effort does not always succeed, at least not to the same degree. By success, I have in mind providing through memory the basis for inner freedom: the ability to make choices consonant with a process of self-formation, which is the making of a set of reasonably integrated life experiences.

To the extent that our life experiences represented in memory are insufficiently integrated to enable us to make decisions—to know what we want, to know what pertains to us and what does not—we have an impaired capacity to choose. This is especially the case when our memories make vivid to us the damaging consequences of acting on our initiative and making choices according to their resonance with the self. When memory, and the emotion it represents, warns us of the damage provoked by self-directed action, it also represents our conviction that our self is impaired in ways that assure using it to guide decisions will inevitably put us in harm's way. When this is the case, the only change that matters is the one that, to borrow Kohut's phrase, "restores" the self to its position in the psyche as the factor capable of integrating experience around a central core.

The *Blade Runner* films embody a theory of change specifically suited to the internal situation just outlined. The goal of change central to the film is to overcome the flaw in the replicant that prevents it from being human: the absence of real memories. The absence of real memories is attributed in turn to the fact that the replicant was made not born and therefore did not have the kind of relationships that integrate around a core of meaning because they express the presence of the self. The changes that will restore the individual's core of being are improvements in the design process, in other words better engineering. Once the improved model is designed and produced, that model, because it can give birth, will release the future generation of replicants from their bondage to humans.

CHAPTER 3

Containment and deliberation

Containment

Inner freedom is not only the freedom to have your thoughts. It is also the freedom to form ideas that integrate thoughts. The purpose of psychoanalysis is not to determine what people think and what ideas they form but to facilitate the free movement of thoughts and the development of the capacity to integrate thoughts by discovering the connections between them. While psychoanalysis is not about providing the individual with direction along a predetermined path, it is about making what he or she does a fuller expression of inner freedom.

By definition, impulse-driven conduct results when the factor that determines what we do cannot be resisted, often when our survival or the survival of those on whom we depend is assumed to depend on immediate action: action before which no thought process can be allowed to intervene. The opposing pole to impulse-driven conduct is self-direction. The self is present in the suspension or negation of the force embedded in the impulse. It is present in the temporal delay that assures acting is not inevitable. Indeed, it would not be incorrect to say that the self *is* the capacity to suspend acting and turn inward. The negation of impulse, the delay before acting, and the thought process that occurs during that delay constitute what we refer to when we speak about self-determination.

If we are to delay action in the presence of powerful impulses to act, certain conditions must be met. These conditions have to do with moderating impulse and strengthening the ability to tolerate having the impulse, and especially the anxiety associated with it, without acting on it. Another way of thinking about moderating impulse is the creation of space for another factor to intervene before acting, the one we refer to as thinking. The idea of engaging the self in conduct refers, then, to an inner function that secures space for thinking.

The term impulse refers to the force powerful emotions have to direct what we do. Children seek to relieve themselves of powerful emotions by transferring them to their parents. This transfer takes place through the expression of emotion directed at the parent. The purpose of this directing of powerful emotions is to communicate a need. The more pressing the need, the more the intent is to have the parent experience the pressure felt by the child, to convey to the parent the child's distress and need for relief from it. This attempt to convey a self-state to the parent can elicit different responses, specifically: withdrawal, retaliation, or containment. Withdrawal and retaliation reject the communication. Containment refers to the process by which the target accepts the communication, takes in the self-state associated with it, then manages that self-state internally, or "contains" it (Bion, 1962).

The attempt to forcibly transfer an emotional state into another person does not recognize self-boundaries and, in that respect, is an act of aggression. Because the transfer of the emotional state involves an act of aggression, the key to containment on the part of the recipient is his or her ability to resist the impulse to retaliate and instead manage the response to the attack internally. Doing so indicates to the source of the aggression that its target has the capacity to survive the attack so that the consequences of the presence in the aggressor of the impulse to attack is not the loss of the relationship and the disastrous consequences implied by that loss. For the child, the relationship with the parent in which states experienced as intolerable by the child are contained by the parent becomes, through internalization, the child's capacity to contain his or her own difficult emotions. Identification with a parent who contains intolerable emotional states becomes an internal object relation that can be called on when the parent is no longer present.

It is, therefore, an essential element in separation from the parent and in the movement in the direction of independent existence.

It needs to be emphasized that containment does not mean repression; nor does it mean turning the aggression directed outward back toward the self. Containment does not block access to our own aggression; rather, it expresses or enacts our knowledge that aggression need not be experienced as a mortal danger to its object and therefore necessitate its repression, externalization, or redirection toward the self. Containment transforms the experience of aggression into something that can be tolerated internally, and therefore into something over which the individual can claim ownership and therefore use.

To make emotion useful in a world of separate persons, emotion must be managed internally, which also means it must be moderated. Moderation requires breaking the equivalence between the emotional interpretation of experience and our understanding of that experience, or, put another way, emotional development means the development of the capacity to know our experience in a new way. For this, we need assistance. Containment is the needed assistance because it opens up space in the inner world not occupied by emotion.

Why do we need to do this? The answer to this question begins with memory: the need to hold experience in our minds and use that experience in determining what we do and how we relate to others. Memories of relationships are held in the form of an internal object or object relation to which an emotional charge is attached. Holding an object in the mind, even one to which an emotional charge is attached, signals the presence there of something more than emotion taken by itself. In other words, it means that emotion is no longer a simple, one dimensional experience so that our memory, for example of our mother, does not correspond to a simple and unchanging experience but corresponds to different and changing experiences. These may be experiences of gratification and of deprivation, and they may be experiences of different kinds and degrees of gratification and deprivation. Emotionally invested experiences can also be attached to objects other than our mother, objects that provide different kinds of experiences.

The problem gains further complexity when the memory is to be used not only in relating within the original relationship out of which it emerged, but also applied to other objects as yet unknown. To use memory to manage our responses to different objects and objects yet unknown we must do some work. This is the work of integrating experience. It is the work of forming abstractions out of concrete experiences, in other words of forming ideas. This work goes on in the mental space created by containment.

The development of ideas out of emotion can be said to moderate emotion by making the interpretation associated with it less one-dimensional and absolute. Moderating the power of emotion also means that it no longer occupies the whole of our mental space; there is room for something else: interpretation and integration. Moderating emotion through the development of internal object relations makes possible the suspension of the impulse embedded in the emotion and thereby creates the possibility of not acting. It thereby establishes the possibility of a mediating process that precedes acting. The inability to create space for this process is expressed in the judgment that something must be done immediately, or the consequences will be catastrophic.

In part, the difficulty moderating emotion poses arises out of the interpretation of the consequences of acting or not acting. The more catastrophic we expect those consequences to be, and the more we take those consequences to be imminent, the less we can delay responding to them and use that delay to moderate our response. Moving the anticipated adverse consequences forward in time expresses the foreshortened temporal frame of intense emotional states. Shifting the time frame mirrors the urgency felt internally, which is the urgency attached to feelings of anxiety about the future and anger directed at those held responsible for anxiety. The latter is the urgency associated with a present-time emotional state and the urgency of the need to relieve it.

This movement forward of the time frame indicates that the problem for which the action insisted on is the intended response is not the problem identified in the external world but the state of anxiety that has been attached to it. Indeed, anxiety about the future is a mechanism for bringing the urgency of action forward in time so that it is now the anxiety itself that is the problem. To the extent that the anxiety arises out of the anticipation that appropriate measures to solve the problem will not be taken, then the problem can be understood as that of the failure of caretakers to identify and respond to an urgently felt problem. This problem may originate outside or it may be associated with the management of the inner world: the need to somehow get rid of bad feelings by evacuating them. Early in life, the failure of the parent's response intensified the bad feelings. Later in life, anticipation of the repetition of that failure together with a limited capacity to manage it internally make present-day challenges reenactments of early failures. Since all anxiety is a response to, or use of, memory, unmanageable anxiety recreates an early experience.

If we bear in mind that anxiety is the way we remember the consequences of early experience, we can see how it becomes the template for present-day anticipations of failure. If this template works poorly in the adult world, then responses to present-day threats shaped by that template are likely to fail, even to exacerbate rather than alleviate the problem. Under these circumstances, what is needed is a new template for experiencing and dealing with the anxiety provoked by real-world events, one that is consistent with the kinds of internal thought processes likely to be effective in an adult world. Following the primitive template, we may need to control those responsible for our intolerable state of mind through projective identification. Following the newer, adult, template, we need to think about a problem and develop meaningful action.

The capacity to move from the primitive experience of anxiety to an adult experience depends on the internalization of a relationship capable of containing emotion. Internalization of an appropriate relationship is, as I have suggested, the basis for self-directed action as an alternative to acting on impulse. Self-direction then depends on the presence of internal object relations in the form both of memories and fantasies through which emotions can be managed without evacuating intolerable emotional states onto others.

Example

A friend I will refer to as Sarah recounted the following experience. During the first two or three weeks of Sarah's analysis, her analyst had been largely silent. He did, however, offer one remark that stuck in her mind. He told her that he understood that she had been doing all the "work" and this was because he needed time to get to know her. For a brief comment of a seemingly mundane sort, what he said had a considerable impact. It prompted a number of thoughts that would remain active throughout her analysis and beyond: that he did not already know much about Sarah but had to learn, and learning about Sarah would take time and effort, and that he understood she might be feeling some urgency and anxiety about the matter. This brief and seemingly innocuous comment became an important memory as the analyst's comment came to represent a part of Sarah's internalized effort to slow herself down, reduce feelings of urgency, open up her mind for an internal process of thinking and learning. I should emphasize that these memories or internal objects did not tell Sarah how to think or what to think, but they did help her allow herself space to think.

Several years into analysis, Sarah was working on a dream. It was complex and somewhat obscure but, by the end of the session, she had made good progress with it. As she was walking out, her analyst commented in passing that during the session he did not think she would "get" it, but she did. His comment set in motion a train of thought. Sarah was surprised at the comment but also agreed that they had both "gotten" it, though also doubtful that they would. In discussing this experience with Sarah, what seemed most important was not what her analyst said, but her response to it, specifically that she believed what he said. This marked a notable moment in her analysis as it meant that she no longer experienced her analyst as already knowing everything about her, but instead as someone who would have to undertake a process of finding out, or learning who she was, a process in which she might also find out about herself.

Some time after my conversation with Sarah, I found myself struggling to help a friend who I will call Bob. Bob suffered from anxiety, anxiety he struggled with but failed to contain. Instead of containing his anxiety Bob transmitted it to others, myself included. I had noticed about Bob that, when I spoke with him, he always spoke very fast barely leaving me room to comment. The experience of speaking with him made me tense even though, in most respects, we had amiable conversations. I felt that the fast talk was blocking me out by assuring that I could not say anything. I wondered if blocking me out was an enactment of an inner drama in which Bob sought to block something internally, something that threatened to emerge were he to slow down and allow time and space for us to connect. In thinking about my experience with Bob, I found myself having a fantasy. In the fantasy, Bob seeks advice from me and asks me if there were one piece of advice I could give him what would it be. In seeking a response to Bob, my conversation with Sarah came to mind prompting the following answer to his question: "Slow down." But Bob could not slow down. He was driven instead by an irresistible impulse to fill the unfilled space.

Deliberation

Containment makes it possible for what we do to be guided by a deliberative process, which, in turn, makes what we do deliberate: an expression of intent rather than impulse. This quality of being deliberate and expressing intent is what constitutes, for the adult, the doing that expresses being. In other words, it makes doing self-directed. For the doing that expresses being there must be this moment of being, which is to say a moment in which the mind sets impulse aside and does nothing, or more precisely does nothing in the outside world. The doing that results from doing nothing no longer expresses urgent and irresistible impulse, but something else: the capacity to assess conduct in relation to anticipated ends and the capacity to assess ends through thinking about them. This is the capacity I associated earlier with choosing. The ends are assessed not according to their capacity to serve impulse, as would be implied by the notion of delayed gratification, but according to their capacity to facilitate being. This also makes it possible to assess being not only for the self but more generally: How do the ends and means facilitate inner freedom not only in the particular case, but more generally.

Deliberation has a public analogue, which is the deliberative process of organizations, including governmental organizations. Decisions in organizations can express the urgency and thoughtlessness we associate with impulse-driven conduct, or they can express the availability of a deliberative process. Thus, the CEO may make decisions unilaterally, based on "trusting his instincts." Trust in instinct means distrust in deliberation, a distrust born of the fear that the outcome of deliberation will differ from the outcome urgently needed. An analogy at the governmental level is the use of popular referenda to make government policy. The outcome of the popular vote does not depend on deliberation. Those voting do not, in general, collect and analyze data as they have neither the expertise nor the time to do so. The result is an impulse-driven decision often with harmful consequences.

An example of the link between anxiety and impulse-driven decision making was provided in the US by the Covid-19 pandemic. One problem posed by the pandemic was communication of information to the public. In doing so, the ideal was a form of communication that conveyed accurate, science-based information about the seriousness of the threat posed by the virus while not provoking the kind of emotional response that fostered a transition from anxiety to panic. It is one thing to be anxious about a trip to the grocery store that has suddenly become a complex, unfamiliar, and potentially life-threatening event; it is something else to find your anxiety rising to a level that undermines your ability to make reality-connected decisions and execute a task necessary for daily life under difficult circumstances. In the former case, we experience normal or limited anxiety, in the latter we experience panic or something close to it. Panic is also a form of anxiety, but not a form that, by signaling danger, enables us to cope with it. This is why a common piece of advice offered during the pandemic was: "Don't panic, prepare." Clearly, panic is the enemy of preparing to cope because it makes the kind of thinking process needed to prepare difficult or impossible to engage.

Yet, it makes little sense to tell people not to panic. Panic is not something anyone chooses to do or can decide not to do. Panic is, rather, a kind of anxiety that defeats the purpose of anxiety, which is to guide us to appropriate self-protective action. Different kinds of anxiety are different emotional interpretations of the threat we face, interpretations formed early in life. The more significant the harm experienced at that time, the more intense the emotions attached to the memory of it, the more anxiety in the present tends to extremes with the resulting impairment in the capacity to think and plan.

Rather than telling people not to panic, what is needed is to offer them a connection with a reliable figure in authority capable of helping them manage their anxiety. But the availability of such a figure will only enable them to manage their anxiety (so it does not turn into panic) if they already have an internalized object relation that can be mapped onto the present-day authority figure. If a suitable internalized object relation is absent either for the leader or for followers, the likelihood of developing and implementing a plan for coping with a real-world crisis and minimizing harm is small.

Thus, in the US, it was clear that, during the pandemic, the president was himself in a state of panic, or near panic. His response to the onset of the pandemic was to deny that it would spread to the US, a denial that allowed him to avoid thinking about it and especially about his responsibility to prepare the country to cope with it, a responsibility for which he was ill-equipped emotionally and intellectually. Rather than plan for the onset of the pandemic, he attacked all those who insisted that it was real and significant, thereby attempting to make the threat to his sense of competence and his fantasy of himself as a leader disappear (Drezner, 2020).

> ... the Trump White House's inadequate handling of the outbreak highlights his every toddler-like instinct. The most obvious one is his predilection for temper tantrums. Some advisers describe an angry Trump as a whistling teapot that needs to either let off steam or explode. Politico has reported on the myriad triggers for his tantrums: "if he's caught by surprise, if someone criticizes him, or if someone stops him from trying to do something or seeks to control him."

It is not democracy that poses the problem, it is the fantasy of democracy: that it needs no deliberative structure to assure that decisions are not based on impulses rooted in fear and desire, but in the goal of protecting safe space in the inner world. Impulse-driven conduct is always based in fantasy, especially the fantasy that the decision between courses of action is a simple binary: the decision between right and wrong, good and bad. All that is needed to make this decision is an inborn moral compass. A compass does not think about alternatives—where is north, where is south—a compass automatically senses direction. It is drawn to point north by an irresistible force.

For the inner world, emotion acts as the magnetic force determining the direction in which our compass guides us. Our moral compass guides us in the right direction when what feels right to us is right. When we trust our emotions, we trust the idea about the world embedded in emotion. Having a moral compass means having the right emotions: care and compassion, gratitude and forgiveness, love. Deliberation does not enter. Use of a moral compass only works, however, if the issues we face in life are as simple as the alternatives identified by our emotions: compassion or indifference, generosity or greed, love or hate. Or, put another way, to make this work, we have to make the issues we face simple binary alternatives. And the more we resist deliberation because it is experienced as a threat, the more we regress to simple binary thinking as a defense against complexity and the need to think.

But the defense against complexity, because it is a defense against deliberation, is also a defense against the self and the use of the self as the basis for determining the path we take. This means that flight from complexity is flight from the self. Thus, in a notable example, the self is identified with greed, so those who are self-directed are understood to be directed by greed and have no moral compass. Rather than having a moral compass that directs them to be concerned for the welfare of others, it is assumed they will always act out of "self-interest." Where there are those in need, for you to think before you act is for you to doubt what you should do, and to doubt what you should do indicates the intervention of powerful forces in your mental life that lead you not to care.

Relating to others and the inner world

Self-directed action, because it depends on the presence in the inner world of an internalized relationship of a special kind, is always the enactment of a relationship. It never develops out of the absence of relating. Further, this relationship is one in which an important need was satisfied by another, so that, in this sense, the individual has been cared for. Failure to be self-directed derives from the failure of care and the absence of a relationship in which we were cared for. This conclusion is reinforced by the observation that those who act out of greed rather than self-interest are typically driven by an overpowering need for other people to take an interest in them, something that did not happen, or did not happen enough when they were growing up. Indeed, it could be said that greed, rather than expressing an excessive interest in the self, actually expresses a deficit in self-awareness and an overly intense interest in others.

The use of the self as an alternative to a moral compass is an indicator of the power of an internalized relationship involving care, while the need for a moral compass indicates deficiencies in internalization of such a relationship and, as a result, the need for an alternative. This means that being self-directed, even self-interested, is a preeminently social condition. It is also the foundation for an internalized capacity to relate to others on a basis other than greed, a basis that takes into account their integrity and their own right to be self-directed. Because self-interest depends on internalization of a relationship in which our emotions are contained rather than exported, it indicates a capacity to recognize self-boundaries.

Self-interest is not social in the sense that it is shaped by cultural norms. Rather, it is social in the sense that it exists only insofar as relationships of a specific kind have been internalized; and they can only be internalized so far as they were available to be used for that purpose. So, our pursuit of self-interest calls on an empathic internal object relation, which makes empathy an essential element in self-interest.

Internalization of the relationship through which emotions are contained constitutes the capacity to relate to others as separate persons. This capacity is the essential element both in establishing internal freedom and in living with others in a way that respects their integrity and therefore in living in a world organized around external freedom. In this sense, external freedom is the expression in relating of the presence of internal freedom.

The capacity for containment makes it possible to relate to others and therefore to live in society. It is the essential element in what is sometimes referred to as "social determination." It is also what we mean by the presence of society in the inner world. But for containment to be effective in this way, it must be possible to generalize or abstract a special way of relating with others so that it does not only apply where relationships are interpersonal, as they are with friends and family members. This generalization or abstraction is, in a sense, already embedded in the process of containment, which is the process by which the capacity to relate to others without presuppositions about them becomes an aspect of psychic life. It is the availability of space in the inner word for thinking without knowing. Internalizing the relationship in which getting to know takes time demands patience, which is to say the absence of the urgency that is the enemy of thinking.

CHAPTER 4

Tradition, group attachment, and stranger anxiety

Tradition

In Chapter 2, I identify freedom with indeterminacy so that what we do is the expression of freedom when it is not predetermined for us or already known to others. The possibility of inner freedom develops in the context of object relations that do not treat us as already known and therefore following a predetermined path. This would seem to make the wish to be already known, as expressed for example in the attachment to tradition, a wish to escape from freedom. Freedom is the problem. Finding a place where we are already known is the solution.

Merriam-Webster (2003) defines tradition as "an inherited, established, or customary pattern of thought, action, or behavior (as a religious practice or a social custom); a belief or story or a body of beliefs or stories relating to the past that are commonly accepted as historical though not verifiable." If traditions are inherited, established, and customary, they are predetermined. Traditions are commonly held beliefs so that attachment to them does not depend on any internal process that would involve thinking about them. Traditions establish cultural continuity by connecting past, present, and future in a way that assures that something essential remains the same across time. We can think of tradition as the embodiment in practice of memories ("stories relating to the past"). Being a conduit for traditions involves using memories of the past to shape what we do in the present.

Yet, this does not mean that freedom has no presence where an attachment to tradition, or to the fantasy of tradition, is also important. Human beings typically express in their lives differing trends imperfectly held together. Even in a world shaped by the fantasy of tradition, freedom can make its presence known, if only in the contingency of the experiences instantiated and interpreted in the traditions of the group and in the possibility that traditions might change over time. This tension is clearly expressed in an exhibition at the Museum of Contemporary Native Art in Santa Fe, NM featuring "New Approaches to Tradition" (Museum of Contemporary Native Art, 2019–2020), and especially in the attempt on the part of the artists featured in the exhibition to make the elements of tradition, especially the symbols that embody it, something personal.

The Museum of Contemporary Native Art is part of the Institute of American Indian Arts. The Institute's stated goal is "empowerment through education, economic self-sufficiency and expression and enhancement of artistic and cultural tradition." It is meant to be "a place where traditions are rediscovered, explored and deepened. Where your art and cultural identity will be celebrated and revered. It is a place of welcome that you will feel part of and will remain part of you no matter how far you go in life." Key elements of the goal that will prove important in understanding the interplay between tradition, memory, and freedom are: to rediscover tradition, to celebrate cultural identity, and to provide a place where students feel a sense of belonging.

This use of tradition as memory can be exemplified in the way tradition appears in the exhibition to which I refer above. I begin with the words used to describe their work by three of the artists represented in the exhibition.

Erin Shaw

My work as an artist rests in the simple assertion: We are collectors of stories and the stories we collect shape the people we are. As I collect and work with stories, I am often reminded that stories are fluid. They must bend and move in order to serve us.

Our ancient stories are vital to us today. To keep them vital, we must actively participate with them. I sometimes see myself going into ancient times, gathering up stories, and bringing them into my current context. Within my work, my aim is not merely a re-telling, but a current engagement—these stories evolve, even as I do. Some imagery is inspired by personal dreams .... In my dream, a mourning dove reached out his wings and handed me a ball. The bird told me, "Your exile was meant to destroy you, but here is your story of return."

Bill Hensley

The inspiration for my work comes from a desire to connect my tribe, my family—our past—to the future .... I often paint using bold colors and various striping techniques. My work is constantly evolving through experimentation with new techniques and mediums, and portraits "woven" into abstract, timeless backgrounds. Traditional imagery and cultural symbols bring Chickasaw culture to the forefront in my artwork, reminiscent of both the rich history of my people, and the story of what it means to be Chickasaw today. Through my work I hope to encourage interest in the Chickasaw people, and a foothold in the global art community. I am inspired by everyday life and the nostalgia it brings, yet the subject of a painting is irrelevant; it is the emotional response to the subject that truly matters.

Brent Greenwood

To establish visual depth in my acrylic paintings, I go through the process of underpainting to create layered effects. Through that process, the work directs me, and I automatically feel that connectedness.

Erin Shaw describes herself as a collector of stories that shape people's lives. These stories occupy the space for the group that memory, and the fantasy that develops out of memory, occupies for the individual. The transition to fantasy is indicated in the fluidity of the "ancient" stories that "bend and move." In telling stories, her intent is not simply to repeat them but to "actively participate with them." In other words, her intent is to enact them in her own way in order to keep them alive. Thus, she makes her life an enactment of the stories she has inherited. The stories, then, solve a problem of living. The more acute the problem, the more remote and unattainable a solution to it seems to be, the more vital the stories become.

In listening to Shaw's account of her work, we hear, among other things, a powerful assertion and insistence on her attachment to ancient stories. As is typically the case, the more powerfully we insist, the more we offer evidence that we are working against resistance, whether internal, external, or both. The greater the need to assert the connection, the more that connection is experienced to be endangered and therefore problematic. Put another way, the language used to speak about the connection tells us that it cannot be taken for granted, accepted without question. We must work to maintain the connection, or the stories will be lost.

Stories can be lost in different ways. First, they can literally disappear, and second, they can lose their significance in people's lives. The same is, of course, true of memories. We may literally lose—forget—our memories; or, while we retain them, they may lose their significance for us. In the second case, we "free" ourselves from them. One danger traditions face is that those who were once attached to the stories will free themselves from them. Insisting on their importance both keeps the emotional connection alive and expresses the presence internally of a movement away from them. Once we stop taking our stories for granted, they are at risk of being forgotten, which is also a metaphor for freeing ourselves from them.

For Shaw, then, the stories are not simply who she is but something on which she needs to insist and make explicit. Not only must she tell the stories in her art, she must tell us that she is telling the stories, and she must tell us that, in doing so, she is telling us about herself. She must assert their importance only because there exists a space between her and the stories, a space she must somehow overcome and at the same time insist on, most notably by creating a uniquely personal image that expresses her connection to them, makes them real for her and for us, while at the same time adapting them to her more personal self.

Reference to ancient stories can convey the history of the group as embedded in them, but it can also connect that history to the member's archaic internal objects experienced as personal memories. Those objects are experienced in memories and, in Shaw's case, in dreams understood through their link with the ancient stories of the group. Thus, they link the psychic lives of members to the cultural reality of the group, thereby merging memory and tradition. Indeed, it can be said that only by finding a link with the individual's personal memories can the group memories become real, can the individual "remember" the past of the group.

For Native Americans, one of the most salient memories is the memory of the experience of the destruction, or attempted destruction, of their people. Through the attachment of the story of attempted destruction to personal memories and dreams, the link to which I have just referred is established. In this sense, it can be said that the individual member of the tribe can be made to remember the tribe's experience as that is instantiated in stories of its past. Here, the salient memory is one of loss, and this memory, through its link with the individual's memory of personal experience, becomes the individual's memory and, as a result, the individual remembers an event he or she never experienced by equating it with an event her or she did experience. This, then, becomes the basis for group solidarity and a group penetration of the individual psyche: "Your exile was meant to destroy you, but here is your story of return."

Bill Hensley echoes this same conviction when he writes that he is driven by his "desire to connect my tribe, my family—our past—to the future." That he paints "abstract, timeless backgrounds" may suggest the timelessness implied in the collapsing of past, present, and future established through forging a connection between what is part of tradition and what is part of the individual's personal life.

Brent Greenwood establishes the same end through underpainting, a process of layering paint that can act as a metaphor for the layering of memories including the layering of personal memories onto the "stories" to which Shaw refers. Allowing a residual of past versions of a painting to appear, however occluded, in the final version can represent the power and presence of memory.

The dream of culture

We can begin to see more clearly the problem to which attachment to tradition offers a solution if we consider a dream recounted to me by a friend I will refer to as Eli. Eli had spent most of his life working in a social justice advocacy organization. Doing so had been a natural extension of his childhood experience growing up in a family where involvement with social justice issues was a significant aspect of family culture. Yet, toward the end of his time with the organization, Eli had come to feel a degree of alienation from it primarily because he did not feel the members or leadership of the organization lived up to the organization's ideals. As this feeling grew, he came to the decision to leave the organization although he knew that leaving it might mean the loss of his sense that there was a place in the world where he belonged.

In Eli's dream, he was entering a building that housed a Jewish organization. As he entered, he noted how beautiful the building was and how his feeling state was imbued with the beauty represented in the building. Once inside, he found himself in a large room arranged for a presentation. There were many chairs, but the room was not crowded. He sat down and found himself next to a young man he had never met. Yet, even though this man was a stranger to him, he also felt that the young man knew him in the way he had most profoundly wished to be known. In the dream, the young man was immediately a very close and reliable friend, the kind of friend he had always wanted to have but thought he would never find. In his dream, Eli felt that finding this young man was the solution to his most deeply troubling problem.

The dream depicts a solution to the problem of disconnection or isolation and the feeling state associated with it. In the dream, the problem of the absence of connectedness is solved while retaining what is essential about being disconnected: finding oneself in a world of strangers. Significantly, in the dream, the feeling state associated with isolation is dispelled without altering the condition within which that state arises. In other words, the solution in the dream involves magical thinking. As it turns out, this magical thinking is bound up with joining a group of a special kind: an ethnic/religious group that Eli was nominally a member of and with which he had a long-dormant association. Although nominally Jewish, Eli had never been involved with Jewish organizations.

Still, he associated his family connection with being Jewish, so he was not altogether surprised that this piece of his identity played the role it did in his dream and in the solution to his problem depicted there.

While we might be tempted to assume that Eli's dream was a response to the isolation he felt having left the organization in which he had spent most of his working life, it is also possible to consider the dream a response to his life *in* the organization and by extension his childhood experience in a world not altogether different from it. The dream, then, embodied the contradiction he experienced in his family and in his work organization: while both claimed to be places where members would be seen or known to each other, they were, in reality, settings where people were strangers to each other. Thus, the leadership in the organization where he had worked typically referred to that organization as a "community," even a "family," suggesting that it offered something to its members that, in reality, it did not. The centrality of the stranger in Eli's dream, and of the magical transformation of the stranger into a friend, suggests that we consider the dream a magical solution to the problem of stranger anxiety (Klein, 1957, pp. 104–105) and that we consider joining certain kinds of groups the pursuit of this magical solution.

The term stranger refers to a person we do not know. The fact that we do not know strangers does not preclude us from relating to and possibly depending on them. The strangers on whom we depend take many forms, but emotionally, so long as they remain unknown to us, they remain incarnations of one entity: the stranger. Strangers provide essential services. And, because we provide them with an opportunity to do their jobs, they also depend on us. So, we are strangers to each other who depend on each other. To be sure, we may at times make friends out of strangers; indeed, for some, doing so is a necessity born of the discomfort they feel relating to strangers. But, so far as we have a sufficient degree of comfort relating to strangers, they can remain strangers even though we depend on them.

Emotionally, the stranger represents the part of the self we keep hidden from others, or, more precisely, the stranger represents our own absent emotional core. Strangers are not "objects" in the psychoanalytic sense of the term: targets of an emotional investment. But, although they are not objects, we can make them objects or relate to them as if they were by projecting our internal objects or object relations onto them.

Indeed, the less actual connection they have with our emotional core, and the less marked the presence of their emotional core in the momentary connection we have with them, the more they operate as an empty container suitable to being filled by our disavowed emotional states.

The qualities that define strangers also encourage a specific kind of projection: the projection of our unknown self. The stranger can be made to represent this unknown self and the ambivalence we feel about it that encourages projection. Ambivalence about the self fosters anxiety associated with the prospect that, should the self become known to others, the defect in the self will be exposed and life-sustaining relationships will be lost. The anxiety we feel about the prospect of exposure can have different sources but one of special importance is anxiety about the absence of a self or emotional core. If the self is absent, or is experienced to be absent, then others who are unknown to us can be made to represent this intolerable reality of ourselves. This is what is "strange" about the stranger: the absence of an emotional core to which a connection can be made. Strangers are experienced to be a threat to the degree that the loss, absence, or impairment of the self originally becomes, through projection, a loss of self in others.

Stranger anxiety arises out of early experiences in which those who would know us (our family members) remain strangers to us, most notably in being physically or emotionally absent or unresponsive. If the original emotional absence was experienced as the loss of an attentive object, able and willing to fulfill our needs, our neediness can appear to be the cause of object loss and, as a result, our seeking or expecting new objects to provide gratification is likely to be felt as a threat to them. If we cannot find an internal template for relating in which new objects are good objects or, in relation to them we are ourselves good objects, our ability to relate to strangers and to work effectively with them can be impaired. In the absence of an appropriate template, new (unknown) objects are always experienced as bad objects, which is to say as sites for the reenactment of a relationship in which we experience ourselves as both aggressors and victims.

Yet, adult life can only be successfully negotiated if we can relate to strangers without an excess of aggression and anxiety. The world outside our family of origin is, or at least begins, as a world of strangers. Whether we seek to get to know those who inhabit this world or we

simply need to be able to interact with them (most notably in work settings), we cannot succeed in having an adult life if the way we relate to
strangers places them into roles in our internal object world that make
them sources of anxiety or targets of aggression.

The magical solution to stranger anxiety activates a wish born in the
experience of family members as strangers with new people we encounter in the world outside the family. After all, the parent who failed to
attend to our emotional needs plays the part of a stranger: someone who
does not know us, who is alien to us, who does not attend to or care about
us. In the solution to this problem offered in Eli's dream, the encounter
with a stranger becomes the return of the lost parent and therefore we
feel that our deepest wish has been fulfilled.

The magic in the dream is the magic that turned the parent from a
bad object into a good object. The magical solution only works so far
as the parent can provide us with a feeling of safety and an experience
of gratification without knowing us, in other words simply by existing,
which is to say by remaining what he or she is: a stranger. In the dream,
the qualities that make someone a stranger to us turn out to be the qualities that define a friend so that seeking friendship becomes seeking after
strangers. In the dream, having overcome his stranger anxiety, Eli would
become the kind of person who finds in strangers a special comfort in
relating provided by those who do not know or get to know him.

This would be facilitated by Eli's finding in a fragment of his early
experience—ethnic identity—the basis for connection. In the magical
solution, this fragment becomes all we need to be fully and intimately
known. In other words, we grab onto a piece of identity attached to us
early in life as a kind of life raft we can hang onto outside the family.
When this internal situation becomes the psychic reality of an ethnic
group, the form of attachment that binds members to it will be significantly shaped by anxiety and strategies employed to manage it. But this
cannot work if the world outside the family is a multiethnic world or
even a world that transcends ethnic identities.

In Eli's case, the significance of the ethnic group stemmed from the
way it represented in childhood a basis for connection within the family
unit, a connection that endured independently of any genuinely personal relationship. To the extent that the problem Eli had within his family was more or less typical of family dynamics within the larger group to

which the family belonged, it is not surprising that he experienced himself as automatically, or at least more easily, connected to the members of this larger group. But this connection, while on first glance comforting, was always based on an ambivalently invested personal experience involving a form of object loss. Within his complex system of internalized object relations and the wishes embedded in them, Eli, through his dream, found a use for traditions he had throughout his life rejected. But the connection found through use of tradition was also a form of disconnection.

Eli's dream can be considered an instance of what Howard Stein refers to as the "dream of culture" (1994). That dream is what must be "preserved" by preserving the salience for us of our culture and the traditions that constitute it. Then, the vital connection offered by culture is the ambivalent connection of childhood, which must be retained or rediscovered outside the family to serve as a basis for adult living and provide the security that was not reliably provided in childhood.

Because it establishes continuity between past, present, and future, the already known (the stories that make up our traditions) must be preserved and protected. We must never forget the stories that bind us together. We must be already known because we cannot live comfortably in a world inhabited by people who are and remain strangers to us. The stories serve to connect members of the group to its past and are used by them in an attempt to integrate the narratives of their personal lives. In the words Shaw uses to describe her dream: "Your exile was meant to destroy you, but here is your story of return."

If we consider the two dreams (Eli's and Erin Shaw's), then we are led to consider the possibility that tradition, as it operates in the modern world, is a dream of return. It is a dream of return to a state of being of the kind Eli both recalled and wished for in his dream: a state of safety and fulfillment. In this state, he no longer experienced his greatest fear: the fear that he had somehow to survive in a world of strangers who were indifferent, if not hostile, to him. What is new about tradition in the modern world is that it must somehow be reconciled with life outside the family, with separation from the kind of attachment we have to traditions so that, in addition to that attachment, we have a new form of attachment in our lives, one in some ways inconsistent with the old.

Eli awoke from his dream in a mildly euphoric state. But this state quickly dissipated as he came to realize that the dream did not offer a solution to his problem but only an expression of the wish for a solution, and the wish for a solution was the opposite of a solution in the same way that the memory of a lost relationship is linked not simply to the good feeling connected to that relationship but also to the bad feeling associated with its absence. So it is with the ancient stories, whether those are stories of the group or of the individual living outside the group in a world that has changed in a way that is not friendly to those stories. Unless the world can be one in which past and present are merged so that the ancient stories are in the present and not just memories of the past, which would be the case if society had not altered in any significant way, the world will not be the world of the stories so that the memories that hold them in the mind are memories of loss and only guides to a future imbued with loss.

When we leave the world of the ancient stories, we leave a way of relating to others that is instantiated in a shared story, in other words, we find ourselves in a world of strangers. We can manage this world in two ways. The first involves transforming it into a world of familial relations: Strangers are treated as if they were friends and, where possible, made into friends. The resulting flight from strangers provoked by stranger anxiety leads us to find a group to replace society or make encounters in society primarily or exclusively encounters with those who are well known to us. Stranger anxiety expresses itself as the obsessive pursuit of friends: the rapid movement from an encounter with a stranger to the recreation of the stranger as a friend. The second is to withdraw from society so far as that is possible so as to avoid the anxiety provoked by relating to strangers.

* * *

A stranger is someone who is not known to us, someone we recognize as like us in being human, but we otherwise experience as unlike us. Being known by others is to have been seen by them before. In the fantasy of the ethnic group, all members have been seen before, even those we have not met. But a friend is something more. A friend is not merely someone previously encountered but someone with whom you have a special relationship, a relationship in which each party is valued by the other. A friend is someone who cares about you and who you care about. Someone you can rely on. To be a friend and to have a friend is to be someone special. In the ethnic group those we have not met are not merely acquaintances, but friends.

In what is sometimes termed a "traditional society," or more precisely in the fantasy of traditional society as that takes form in the modern world, others are already known to us and valued by us. No one depends on strangers for their well-being or cares about them. What happens to them does not matter. In such a society, children matter to their parents only insofar as they are not strangers. To be cared about, children must be already known, from birth or even before birth. It therefore becomes important that children confirm that they are what they are already known to be, what they are independently of any distinct or personal trajectory of life. Using the language of *Blade Runner 2049* children are made not born.

To the extent that this is the case, and it will typically be a matter of degree, adaptation to an identity already known makes choice in the sense discussed in Chapter 1 not only impossible, because the basis for it in personal identity does not exist, but inconsistent with the demands of belonging. To have to make choices is to confront stranger anxiety because making choices that shape your life will make a stranger of you; in Bollas' language, it will bind you not to your fate but to your destiny. Thus, the link between choice and a personal trajectory of development that can act as the basis for choosing implies that the capacity for making choices rests on the absence, or at least weakness, of the fear of strangers and of the urge toward flight from a world they inhabit.

Stranger anxiety is inherent in a society where the development of the child means the taking on of an already determined identity. This is because to be predetermined is to have what is personal and unique about you ignored or devalued. Stranger anxiety develops outside the setting of a society organized around tradition when parents cannot tolerate the separate being of their children, which is their being for themselves rather for their parents. Where the opportunity to discover a personal or separate being was not afforded parents in their development, it will be difficult for parents to nurture that discovery in their children. As a result, stranger anxiety, whether it expresses itself in avoiding strangers or in the compulsion to make friends out of them, will be transmitted across generations. The issue is not whether we seek or avoid strangers, but whether we tolerate their remaining strangers in our relations with them, which is to say their remaining different from and indifferent to us.

CHAPTER 5

Willful change

Choice and change

An emotional investment in the possibility of making changes in our lives originates in the same experience of the inner world we associate with choice. If we can choose, we can also choose differently. That possibility is implied in choosing. We might choose differently because new options become available. But new options become available because the world is organized in a way that includes choosing differently. If it were not, all new options would fail, and, indeed, the inner impetus for developing and offering new options would not be present.

There are, of course, imposed changes to which we must adapt, changes as varied as growing old and global warming. These changes are not invented to express the freedom we associate with choice; they arise due to factors having nothing to do with those that underlie choosing. Still, the possibility of adapting to them by inventing or discovering new ways to lead our lives consistent with imposed change can call on the inner resources we associate with choice and the kinds of changes the presence of those factors make possible.

To the extent that change and choice have a common origin, it will not be surprising that those living in a world where the factors associated with choice predominate will think of change as the expression of choice. The idea of willful change captures this link between change and choice by treating the former as something we can decide to do at our will. The factors that lead us to treat change as a choice originate early in the individual's emotional development at a time when the personality is in the process of taking shape. There is a sense in which, early on, there are relatively few limits to what we can become because the personality has yet to take shape and the self exists primarily as a potential, not as the realization of that potential in a life of a particular kind. Rather than saying that there are few limits, however, it may be more accurate to say that the limits are not yet known. Even so, not knowing who we will be and what limits our decisions will set for us means that we operate with fewer constraints the earlier in the process we find ourselves.

Winnicott speaks of the earliest experience of this absence of limits when he speaks of the "infantile illusion" of having the capacity to "create the world" (1986). The world the infant creates, or imagines him- or herself to create, is not, however, a world of choices but of an undifferentiated unit in which all the infant's needs are satisfied. There are no choices here, and no need to exercise the capacity for making choices.

That choice and the capacity to choose come later is implied in their link to thinking. Thinking requires the presence of something to think about, in this case, the possible alternative courses of action. As we have seen, these can be provided from outside or internally generated. Thinking can also create choices. This happens because thinking takes place during a pause in acting. During this pause, there is room for the discovery of alternatives, something that is not possible when action is wholly impulsive.

Thinking both opens up alternatives and limits options. This is, in part, because thinking differs from imagining: the fantasy process by which the restraints associated with reality are suspended. As opposed to fantasy, thinking is an engagement with reality through which we seek to discover alternatives not yet thought although in some sense implied in what already exists. The sharpest limits reality places on our thinking process require that we limit thinking to choosing among already known alternatives. But creative thinking is also possible. While creative thinking has features in common with fantasy, the two differ in the way scientific advance differs from science fiction: Creative thinking seeks to discover features that are in reality but not yet known while fantasy makes things up independently of any constraints placed on what is possible by what exists or can exist. The made-up alternatives of fantasy connect fantasy to desire: Fantasy is shaped by what we wish reality was rather than by what reality could be. Thinking applies when reality contains within it possibilities not yet known. When we deny that this is the case, then reality is not the setting of the possible, but an obstacle to it. For there to be something different we must get rid of reality, which is what the fantasy process does for us. There are, then, two kinds of change: the change that brings to awareness what is hidden, and yet implicit, in reality, and the change that dismisses reality so that fantasy can be put in its place.

Thinking and choosing emerge when the parent does not already know who the child will become but, at least to some degree, leaves the matter up to the child to determine. Then, a new capacity develops: the one I have described as testing alternatives for consistency with the self. The process of making choices is the process of forming the self into a particular person with particular interests and capabilities. We give up our ability to create *the* world so that we can live in *a* world, one uniquely our own. We then live in this world of our own that is also embedded in the world outside: a world that we do not create and over which we do not exert the omnipotent control we associate with fantasy. This embeddedness of our world in a world outside that is given to us can cause problems. The difference between the two can be taken to diminish the importance of our private world in ways we have a hard time tolerating. At this point, an impetus to bring about change in the world outside can become an important motivation for what we do.

The early process of self-formation differs from the process of making choices so far as the young person cannot call on past experiences and memories of them to guide choosing. Everything is new; suitable memories are yet to be made. This does not mean that early in life there is no basis for doing and relating. Here, rather than recourse to a well-defined self as the basis for making decisions, there is the process of identification. At this early stage in life, identification offers a solution to the problems: Who am I? What will I be? The answer is: I will be what my parents (and others with whom I have the opportunity to form an identification) are. This solution is not applied willfully, however, but independently of the young child's willing and choosing.

The movement from identification to choice involves a gradual intervention of thinking about the self as the basis for acting. Thinking loosens primitive identifications, though it does not altogether overthrow them. The process of loosening primitive identifications is facilitated by the growing number of objects available for identification and the resulting increase in the number of objects internalized, as expressed in the increasing wealth of salient experiences instantiated as memories. Thus, according to Erik Erikson:

> The limited usefulness of the *mechanism of identification* becomes at once obvious if we consider the fact that none of the identifications of childhood ... could, if merely added up, result in a functioning personality .... The final identity, then, as fixed at the end of adolescence is superordinated to any single identification with individuals of the past: it includes all significant identifications, but it also alters them in order to make a unique and reasonably coherent whole of them. (Erikson, 1959, pp. 120–121)

The better integrated the result of this process, the more the individual will be able to choose based on a known, integrated, and well-defined self. Rather than deciding what to do based on a single identification, there is the possibility of choice. But, as the basis for choice becomes well-established, the possibility for change diminishes. The possibility for change diminishes because the larger decisions that shape a way of life and give form to the self as the center of decision making have already been made and are now not the object whose formation is the end of choosing, but the core of being we have reference to in making choices. Thus, the presence of a fully formed capacity to make choices limits the possibility of change to changes that do not alter the now well-formed choosing agent.

In this connection, consider Samuel's experience of difficulty with his career choice discussed in Chapter 1. There, I highlighted two factors blocking Samuel from experiencing his profession as something he chose to enter: a problem with self-knowledge and a problem with making an emotional investment in a career path. In light of the above remarks, we can also consider a third possibility: the possibility that Samuel's dissatisfaction with the way he went about arriving at his career is an expression not of deficiencies in the way he approached the problem at the time, but of present-day regret that he cannot return to or revive the moment in his life when options were many and the future yet to be determined, in other words a time when he was a potential and not a fully formed person. This is not so much a desire for career change, although it can be experienced that way, as a desire to return to an earlier state, a desire that could not be satisfied by career change, or by anything else for that matter. In the language used above, Samuel was lamenting the impossibility of willful change.

Samuel's emotional reaction to the loss of possibilities yet to be deter-mined was a limited one. He felt regret but did not enact the wish to undo what had been done and escape from the consequences of his past decisions. For some, however, the response to the loss of, or prospect of loss of, possibilities yet undetermined is more intense and radical. For them, it takes the form of a commitment to willful change in adult life. The continuing commitment to willful change in the adult represents a rebellion against the limits created by a life trajectory. It involves the insistence that taking form is not inevitable or enduring, which is also the insistence that we can live a life as an unformed potential and make decisions without any firm foundation for doing so. This treats decision making as the direct or unmediated expression of desire, a kind of vis-ceral urge rooted in a pure being uncontaminated by its history or by any need to become anything in particular.

Two factors sponsor rebellion against accepting the finitude of the self: doubts about the self that make it a problematic source for deci-sion making, and identifications that include, as a significant element in them, an attack on the self. These factors together make it difficult to integrate, and to some degree transcend, identifications so that the result of personality development can bear the imprint of the self.

One possible expression of the resulting internal situation is false creativity. False creativity appears as a powerful urge to differentiate what the self produces from all that came before, most notably from the identifications that represent the internalization of past relationships and experiences. For the individual driven by the urge to false creativity, what appears as a creative urge—to produce something new—is, in reality, the urge to destroy something old. By destroying the old, it is imagined that it becomes possible to take possession of the world. And, for those driven by the urge to false creativity the purpose of creativity is not to produce something in the world, but to provide definitive proof to self and other of the existence of the self, something the individual driven to false creativity cannot take for granted. It is not to *produce* anything but to *be* something, not to experience real existence, but to create the belief in self and other that you are real when you doubt that is the case.

Taking possession of the world means taking the world away from those who are perceived to possess it. Taking possession of the world, therefore, requires its destruction. The end is to destroy identifications and the external containers for the object relations that is their residue in the personality. The result is an attack on existing as a way of purging them from the inner world and ridding that world of their destructive power.

The sense that there exist limitlessness possibilities can result from a refusal to accept any fixed and limited form, in other words from the hatred of limits. The hatred of limits is the child's response to the reality principle, specifically to the discovery that there is a distinction between *the* world and *her* world, a world over which she exerts control and a world over which she does not. The news of this distinction arrives with the related news that her world is a small part of this other world, and that *the* world impinges on her world in unwelcome ways. A natural response to this news is simply to reject it. This rejection may take the form of denial, but it can also take the form of an attack on the unwanted world and the power it wields against the infantile illusion.

When this rejection remains powerful into adulthood, it can take the form of the demand for change in the world that would align it better with the wished-for world that has been, if not lost, radically diminished. Then, the power to create the world is not given up but exercised as the power to change the world so that it accords better with the fantasy that the world is fungible in the same way that the personality of the child is experienced to be. By contrast, for those whose personalities have settled into a well-defined form and have come to terms with the limits implied in the reality principle, the limits of change are more apparent and prominent in their thinking.

A prominent part of the struggle with limits is likely to be a struggle with greed, which represents the denial of limits. Hatred of limits reflects the power of greed in the personality. The danger posed by greed as an attack on reality, especially the separate reality of the parents, means that greed must be managed, most notably by projection. The more powerful the hatred of limits, the more potent the power of greed in the personality and the more potent the impulse to find external containers for greed, which then become targets for aggression.

The Green New Deal

As an example of the hatred of limits, consider a US legislative proposal advanced regarding the problem of climate change. This proposal—the Green New Deal or GND—would lead to sweeping and profound changes in the existing economic and social system (Green Party US, n.d.). The GND is an interesting case in point because it is both a fantasy, the "Green Dream" as the speaker of the US House of Representatives put it, and a proposal whose urgency and scope are not out of proportion with the seriousness of the problem with which the proposal is meant to deal. The fantasy element resides precisely in the dismissal of the limits of reality to what can be done to bring about changes that may in fact be desirable.

Central to the proposal is dealing with the challenge of climate change: "We propose an ambitious yet secure economic and environmental program that will revive the economy, turn the tide on climate change, and make wars for oil obsolete—allowing us to cut our bloated, dangerous military budget in half." The GND is not limited, however, to meeting the challenge of climate change. In addition to dealing with climate change, the GND would be "a major step towards ending unemployment for good," and "a tool to fight the corporate takeover of our democracy and exploitation of the poor and people of color" (Green Party US, n.d.).

Specifically, the GND would "move the country to 100% clean energy in ten years." It would "create a Commission for Economic Democracy to provide publicity, training, education, and direct financing for cooperative development and for democratic reforms to make government agencies, private associations, and business enterprises more participatory."

Thus, the Green New Deal would not only respond to the climate crisis, it would also "strengthen democracy via participatory budgeting and institutions that encourage local initiative and democratic decision-making." Additionally, the GND would "end unemployment in America once and for all by guaranteeing a job at a living wage for every American willing and able to work." The GND would also transform cities by "retrofitting, mass transit and 'complete streets' that promote safe bike and pedestrian traffic, regional food systems based on sustainable organic agriculture, clean manufacturing, infrastructure, and public services (education, youth programs, childcare, senior care, etc.). Communities will use a process of broad stakeholder input and democratic decision making to fairly design and implement these programs."

The magnitude of the changes that would be brought about by the GND is commensurate with the magnitude of the threat to which the program is intended to respond:

> Our nation—and our world—face a "perfect storm" of economic and environmental crises that threaten not only the global economy, but life on Earth as we know it. The dire, existential threats of climate change, wars for oil, and a stagnating, crisis-ridden economic system require bold and visionary solutions if we are to leave a livable world to the next generation and beyond .... The fate of humanity is in our hands. It is not just a question of what kind of world we want, but whether we will have a world at all.

The GND is meant to do nothing less than bring about radical change in ways of life. It is necessary to do so because, if we do not, our world will no longer provide us with a livable environment. If the "world" is the environment in which we live, and if the way we lead our lives is rapidly making our world unlivable, then we must radically alter the way we lead our lives, which means that we must radically change who we are. And we must do so by an act of will. In this respect, the GND is willful change writ large.

The goal is to remake the world from a threat to life to a place that sustains life. Underlying this impulse is the idea that ways of life are fungible, in other words, there is no significant investment, emotional or otherwise, in the existing way of life. This may, to some extent, be true early in the process of personality formation. But, beyond that early stage, as we have seen, holding on to the idea that identity, and therefore way of life, is always fungible expresses the presence of a powerful wish that we can always remake ourselves, a wish that has roots in a profound dissatisfaction with the person we have become, a dissatisfaction that can then be projected onto the world outside. When it is projected in this way, the world comes to represent the locus of our dissatisfaction. A proposal that in many ways offers useful ideas about change can simultaneously serve as a vehicle for this dissatisfaction, and, when it does, those who advance it can lose track of the distinction between what is desired and what is possible. Then, the belief that we can fix what is unsatisfying about the world becomes the belief that, by an act of will, we can fix what is unsatisfying about ourselves.

That identity can easily change runs into difficulty, represented in the GND proposal by its treatment of the matter of infrastructure, which must be torn down and replaced if the dire consequences of climate change are to be averted. Insistence that we can transition to clean energy sources is insistence that the infrastructure built to facilitate the current sources can be easily and quickly replaced—in ten years—by a radically different infrastructure. To do this, the existing infrastructure of cars, airplanes, trains, trucks, and buses would need to be replaced, existing power plants replaced along with much of the electrical grid. Specifically, in a plan closely related to the GND, a senator and presidential candidate proposes to "replace or scrap all aircraft, the vast majority of cars and trucks, most buses, trains and ships; hundreds of power plants; and much of the electrical grid—which is what he would have to do to reach his promised '100 percent renewable energy for electricity and transportation'" (von Drehle, 2019).

Here, infrastructure represents the physical embodiment of a way of life, the way it becomes something tangible and enduring rather than something fungible, even ephemeral. The infrastructure of energy production acts as a stand-in for the infrastructure of our emotional lives built up over the years in and through activities and relationships. This emotional infrastructure consists in the system of internal objects and object relations instantiated in memories and fantasies, a system of knowledge and expertise for our work life in which we have made an emotional investment.

If the infrastructure of our lives together is fungible in the way implied by the GND, then so also is our internal infrastructure. Or, more precisely, we assume the external infrastructure is fungible because of our hope that our internal emotional infrastructure is. We are not stuck with what we are and what we have. If we are not stuck with our identity, we are not stuck with the self our identity represents and embodies as a way of life. In sum, the emotional meaning of the GND is that commitment to a way of life is a choice and can therefore be altered by choice.

But, if this is not the case, the proposed changes would put people in an alien world from which they cannot escape. This world is alien in the sense that existing identifications and ways of thinking about self and others do not apply there. Because they do not apply, they no long afford people any guidance in how to lead their lives. As a result, they are set loose from their moorings, adrift in a world that lacks meaning for them. In light of this, the possibility should not be dismissed that setting people adrift is part of the intent of the GND. To the extent that that is the case, the GND constitutes an act of aggression. And, while overtly this is meant to be aggression against greedy corporations, it is also, and more importantly, an act of aggression against all those people who have built up over time commitments to ways of life that bear sufficient meaning for them that to lose those ways of life would cause significant emotional harm.

The advocates of the Green New Deal see in particular problems— climate change, unemployment, failure of democracy, inequality— symptoms of a larger illness: greed. So, what is needed is a revolution: the destruction of the world and its replacement by a new world, one without greed. Yet, while the GND is an attempt to deal with the catastrophic consequences of human greed, the response can also be considered a form of greed. Theirs is a greed to have and to live in a newly made world. This greed is expressed both in the attack on the world they inherited and in their preoccupation with greed's external container: private, for-profit corporations. The global aspirations for change indicated suggest their dissatisfaction with any finite or limited changes, which is to say changes limited by the continuing existence, to whatever degree, of the world as it is. What Emile Durkheim (1897) refers to as the disease of the infinite is always present where willful change has no limits and it is assumed that the defects in the world can be fixed by an act of will, in this case the passage and implementation of the GND.

The advocates of the GND and those who consider it a dream see change differently both in its goals in the ways it can be achieved. The latter consider change that operates within the constraints of the reality that has been built up over a long process of evolution. Taking the analogy with the individual, they are considering the kind of change that is possible for an adult, more or less fully formed, while the GND rejects the idea that maturation of an individual or a social system sets limits to what it can become.

Inner freedom and external reality

In line with their description of the future without the GND, its advocates speak about partial or gradual responses that accept the prospect of living in a more limited world, and living with the inevitable disasters and suffering that are likely in that world, as no better than doing nothing at all. This understanding of the alternatives mirrors a psychic reality of the child for whom bad experiences can rapidly become unmanageable and life threatening. When this psychic reality is well established as an organizing principle of the inner world, there is no middle ground in response to threats, perceived or real. The memory of the early catastrophe now shapes the meaning of the one that is imminent.

This internal threat is the destruction of inner space or, more specifically, the loss of inner freedom. The reality principle should mean the expansion of both internal and external space. But for many it means the expansion of external space at the expense of internal.

Shrinking of the external world due to climate change and the greed that brought it about corresponds to an internal world in which there is no space to live because of the experience of the self as the center of greed and the cause of the destruction of the world, which is the loss there of a benevolent force capable of assuring emotional health and survival. An internalized relationship with a parent who rejects expressions of presence and responds to the need for attention as a greedy attack becomes an internal prohibition on the pursuit of gratification.

This internal prohibition then gets projected outside and the real threats to the external world become enactments of the internal.

The result is that limited solutions are viewed as half-measures that, rather than preventing catastrophe, legitimize the behavior that leads to that result. From the point of view of the emotional configuration of the inner world, there are no choices, we must do what must be done or the world will cease to be a place in which it is possible to live. Anything less is not an option. From the standpoint of both the internal and external worlds, there is a certain truth in this judgment. But there is also a truth denied in it, which is that the world (both internal and external) has evolved in such a way that survival is unlikely. Yes, something must be done to make the inner world a place in which it is safe to be; but this does not mean that something can and will be done.

This suggests a connection between inner freedom and the recognition of limits. The more we pursue the know-no-limits freedom to remake the world, the less we accept the limits that make our freedom something that exists in finite reality. Rather, freedom means the destruction of reality. Freedom can only create in fantasy, never outside. Inner freedom and the freedom to have a life are in conflict. It is the freedom to create plans that can never be and to reject the process that could make something real because the product does not dismiss the inevitability of a tragic outcome. The wish embedded in this alternative freedom is the wish to be free of memory, free of internalized object relations that shape and limit who we are and what we can do. It is the wish to be free for the experiences and the emotional investments that make us who we are, in other words that constitute our "reality."

CHAPTER 6

Recording memories

A record of the self

While we think of memories as experiences contained in the mind, external objects can also be involved in memory. In particular, there are external objects that, like memory, are capable of resonating emotion. To recall an event, or call a memory to mind, whether by intent or not, is to call to mind an emotion attached to or embedded in the memory of the event. In some cases, the experience of recalling memories gets bound up with the process of creating objects with the power to provoke emotions. When this is the case, the creative act is meant to be an act not only of creating something new, but of recalling something from the past.

Consider, in this connection, the photographer W. Eugene Smith. Smith began his career as a photojournalist. In that capacity, his most notable work was done on the front lines during WWII, where he not only recorded the suffering of war, but also experienced that suffering when he was seriously injured by mortar fire. His work during the war and after he returned was distinctive for the intensity of emotion provoked by his images, an intensity produced by the way the darkness of the images was punctuated by highly contrasting lighted sections, and by the powerful emotions of the subjects expressed in their facial expressions and the orientations of their bodies.

As a result of his work both before and during the war, Smith had become a highly regarded photographer working most notably for *Life* magazine. Conflict with the editors of the magazine, specifically over control of the layout of his images, made it impossible for him to continue their association. The same conflict eventually made it impossible for him to make a living as a photojournalist. The conflict over editorial control expressed a deeper conflict over meaning. The presentation of images was not a simple aesthetic matter but engaged the question of what it all meant. Taken together, the images were meant to tell a story. In designing the presentation of his work, Smith sought to make his images fit into what one of his biographers, Sam Stephenson, refers to as "the storytelling situation" (2017, p. 35). When Smith and the editors at *Life* clashed, this was a clash over the meaning embedded in the story line. To Smith's way of thinking, only he knew what that meaning was and only his layout would be true to it.

This conflict did not take the form of an argument about ideas, and it is unlikely that Smith could have put the meaning embedded in his story line into words. Over time, the nonverbal quality of the meaning Smith intended his images to convey led him away from narrative and "toward image and poetry." The result was what Stephenson refers to as "meditative visual sequences" (p. 40). Stephenson describes this transition in relation to a project entitled *The Big Book*, a book that contained no text: "What matters most in the *Big Book* are shapes and rhythms, patterns of tones, and an underlying sense of the foibles of human culture—the hungry, blind, march toward death, often at the political and economic hands of fellow humans" (p. 43). The movement in the direction of meditative visual sequences brought Smith closer to his object: the creation of a resonator of memory and of the emotions embedded in it. His movement in this direction constituted regression away from more advanced modes of communication, which, in turn, brought him closer to making contact with primitive experience.

There was, I suspect, a danger in this regression: the danger of fragmentation or the loss of the adult capacity to integrate experience through the thinking process. This loss does not necessarily represent a flaw in Smith's method. On the contrary, it may be a strength. But to the extent that the trend in his work expressed an ongoing fragmentation of Smith's inner world, regression would, over time, pose a serious, even mortal danger to him. The thinking process makes explicit the links between the seemingly disparate thoughts, feelings, memories, and fantasies that make up the content of the mind.

Thoughts, memories, fantasies, and the emotions with which they are bound up are integrated by their connection to a core of meaning and purpose. When this core is damaged in some important respect or when the individual is unable to gain access to it in shaping conduct and relating, the individual comes to feel that the world has lost meaning and that he or she has no sense of purpose in living. In Smith's case, this situation eventuated in a life devoted to the search for meaning. But the search in the external world for his emotional core was, by definition, doomed to fail, and, in failing, sponsor the endless repetition that was his experience of living his life. Thus, while, to those outside, Smith appeared to be driven by an overwhelming purpose, his obsessive activity—working through the night and often going days with little sleep—is better understood as the expression of a deficit in his emotional core.

What can we say about the memories that shaped the state of mind resulting from Smith's regression from the internal process of finding meaning to the search in the external world? While our information is limited, three events in Smith's life stand out: the death by suicide of his father, his early relationship with his mother, and his traumatic experience in the war. Smith's photography can be considered an ongoing effort to record these experiences, in other words, to record the past through present-day images. The past he sought to record was one marked by a dead father and a "domineering and stern" mother possessed of an indomitable will that was both "grim and authoritative" (p. 12).

Smith was strongly identified with his mother, who was also a photographer. Both his work in photography and the willfulness of his attitude toward his employers can be considered aspects of this identification. We can get a sense of the quality of Smith's internalized maternal relationship from the following vignette. One day, Smith was walking around his loft with an eyeball shaped crystal around his neck.

When asked by a friend how he might acquire one like it, he told the following story that he attributed to Tennessee Williams:

> I have to find a gypsy first. Actually, it was the eye of her daughter. It had a tear in it. It took a year and a half for her to build a tear. When she had an emotion, which wasn't often, she would take this eye and she would squeeze it. And one tear would drop out, and because it was so rare, so precious in this callous little witch, it became like a precious stone, jewel of a tear. And kings fought mighty battles and killed millions to gain this precious stone. (pp. 47–48)

The crystal he was wearing carried a powerful significance involving a "callous little witch" and the profound difficulty of eliciting a single expression of emotion from her. The story suggests both how difficult it was to elicit an emotional response in one of his most significant primary relationships and, at the same time, how impaired he was by the internalization of that relationship in making contact with his own emotional core. As we will see, this impairment became a central feature in his involvement with street photography later in his life. We can also speculate that there is a connection between the emotional meaning of the story and the way Smith was drawn to the front lines in WWII.

The complex identifications Smith formed early in life are also expressed in an image taken in 1951 entitled "Wake of Juan Carlo Trujillo" (Magnum Photos, n.d.). The photograph depicts the body of an old man laid out on a bed with a group of women mourning his death. The image is almost entirely dark but punctuated by bright highlights especially on the face of one young woman. In the image we see several figures that can be considered aspects of Smith's identifications with his parents: the dead man, who is the center of attention for the other figures, the women mourning his death, and especially one young woman who is the center of attention of the photograph. Given his strong identification with his mother, we should consider the possibility that this young woman represents Smith's internalized mother. Thus, the image represents figures with whom Smith is powerfully identified, especially a dead father and a mother absorbed in the darkness of mourning.

The idea that the images in his photographs represent not an attempt to record something outside, but rather an attempt to record the reality of his inner world is strongly supported by the method of work Smith employed. Smith spent hours in the darkroom creating his images. This work in the darkroom was essential to the creative goal Smith pursued. The photographer Jim Karales, who, for a time, worked closely with Smith, observes that "at least fifty percent of the image is done in the darkroom—I think Gene would say ninety percent" (Stephenson, p. 33). For Smith, the negative "can't produce the image completely as the photographer saw it—not as Gene saw it" (p. 33). In thinking about Smith's photography, it is important to keep in mind the complex relationship between creating, remembering, and recording embedded in his method, which both recorded and created an event much as the individual produces a memory both by recording and by creating. The creative part adapts the original image as the camera produced it to the fantasy driving the photographer when he took the photograph.

Stephenson captures something important about Smith's memory creation when he describes his darkroom technique in the creation of an image of an African American midwife birthing a baby in rural South Carolina: "Using his idiosyncratic darkroom shading techniques, Smith visually swaddled and caressed these two caregivers, innocent he felt in a way he wasn't. He exalted them, loved them, created odes to them" (p. 20). They were, in Stephenson's words, "caressed by shadows," just as darkness was a powerful presence when Smith was caressed by his mother. While it may be that he envied the innocence in the photograph, this may also be a photographic recreation of his experience of his relationship with his mother, one that simultaneously captured both being loved and cared for and being surrounded by darkness. Many of his photographs, most notably in the series "Country Doctor" (Magnum Photos, n.d.), convey a powerful theme of care and concern as, in its way, does the photograph "Wake of Juan Carlo Trujillo." Many of these images suggest the presence of a powerful concern, most notably concern for life itself: its fragility, its vulnerability, and its loss.

Smith's internalized relationship with his father also plays an important part in the prominence of shadow in his work and in his life. How this might be the case is suggested by his work during the war.

Working in the army as a photojournalist did not inevitably mean working at the front lines. Smith, however, sought that assignment and the dangers, both physical and emotional, implied by it. More specifically, he sought the raw material the front lines provided for the images he needed to make. Smith "fed off risk" and had a "cavalier" attitude toward his work in combat zones (p. 22). While under mortar fire, he stood up because only by doing so could he get the shot he needed. The result was grievous injury.

Smith described himself as feeling alive when he put himself at risk. But it could also be something darker: the seeking after an experience of death, whether vicarious or real. His photographs, then, insofar as they conveyed concern for vulnerability and fragility could express his inability to care for himself, his loss of access to a factor in his personality, built out of an identification with one of his parents, that is able to keep his self or spirit alive and well.

It is in this connection that his father's suicide becomes significant. On the day he killed himself, his "father drove to a hospital parking lot two miles from their home on the riverbank and blew open his stomach with a shotgun" (p. 18). The analogy with war and war injury is, I think, striking, and suggests that Smith's pursuit of images that could only be taken during combat was not simply an attempt to feel alive, but also an identification with the act by which his father brought about his own death. Smith's photography was, then, the pursuit of a record (memory) of his father's death, which, in the limit, became an attempt to record, and thus assure he could hold onto, the memory of his own death, as paradoxical as that may seem. Indeed, had he not survived his injuries, the photograph he took at the moment the mortar that caused his injury exploded would have been a photograph of his death. The photograph itself contains nothing but the visual image of an explosion, something that is also consistent with his depiction of himself as a "volcano on the verge of eruption" (p. 25).

Smith survived the war, but not without serious injury, both physical and emotional. The same could be said, at least with regard to emotional injury, about survival of his childhood, one result of which was the development within him of a volcano on the verge of eruption, an intensity of emotion that expressed itself most notably in the destruction of his ties to his family and the destruction of his career. The presence of powerful self-destructive impulses, rather than a capacity to care for the self, expressed itself late in life in the form of his addiction to drugs and alcohol, and a lifestyle devoid of any enduring experience of love.

This intensity of emotion implied in the metaphor of the volcano contrasts sharply with the effort required to elicit one single tear from the "callous little witch" in the story represented by the crystal. The intense emotion represented by the volcano could only be brought under control by an intense effort of repression, a repression so intense that it took a Herculean effort to elicit one small emotional expression.

* * *

Eventually, Smith abandons his family and moves into a dilapidated loft in the Flower District of Manhattan. During his time living in his loft, the subject of his camera work focused on the everyday lives of people on the street. We can gain insight into the complex process of the creation of memories in which Smith was engaged if we consider the way in which he took many of his photographs. Sitting on the windowsill of his loft, looking down on the street, he photographed people as they went about their daily activities. Thus, while he could see his subjects, they did not see him and were therefore unaware a photograph was being taken. While attempting to capture their emotional lives, his stance was remote and impassive. In the act of capturing an image of a stranger, Smith was enacting an internalized relationship with his parents. Could we say that, to them, he was a stranger observed from a distance? Was this their attitude to Smith's emotional life as a child? Was this Smith's attitude toward his own emotional life?

Because his subjects are strangers, the emotions Smith records are not memories, but fantasies associated with objects: the photographs. The distinction is typically overlooked in street photography, which is thought to be an example of realism in photography. However, a recent revelation concerning a famous photograph taken by Alfred Eisenstaedt suggests that we reconsider our assumptions about realism in photography. This is the iconic photograph "V-J Day in Times Square." The photograph captures a kiss between a young woman and a soldier returning from the war and has been taken by those who view it as an image of the reunion of two lovers separated by war, which is, indeed, the case *in fantasy*. But, in reality, the photograph is a record of a physical assault by a stranger (Hesse, 2019). This dissonance exists for all street photography, if not always in the dramatic form it takes for Eisenstaedt's image. Because Smith is photographing strangers, the emotions he records are not memories, but nor are they records of the realities of the lives of his subjects, realities of which neither he nor the viewer of his images has any knowledge. This means that, as "realistic" as Smith's images are, they are better understood as fantasies: the attempt to capture something of his own inner world in the world outside.

The images Smith shoots are nothing more than the raw material out of which he creates the record of his own fantasy life, a record that has the appearance of reality when instantiated in his photographs, in other words the appearance of memories rather than fantasies. He shoots tens of thousands of images, creates proofs, pins them on his walls, and spends his time in the obsessive search for and creation of the image that conveys the message, even story line, for which he is searching, just as the viewer of the Eisenstaedt photograph sees in it what he or she wants or needs to find there.

Over time, Smith fills his loft with images of a lost and wished-for life in which strangers appear as actors playing the roles of the central figures. Smith shoots tens of thousands of images and covers his walls in the hope that he will find among them the reality of his wished-for self: a real person engaged in the mundane activities of a real life, often sad, sometimes concerned, occasionally compassionate. The loft is a setting removed from reality, a place from which he can record a reality outside in the hope of finding there the hidden meaning of his life.

The impetus behind his photographic work reveals itself in related activities of recording. He makes audio recordings of conversations, music, stray sounds. By the time he leaves his loft he has in his possession hundreds of thousands of prints and negatives and 1,740 reels of audio tape (O'Hagan, 2017). An obsession with recording is also an obsession with loss and with employing physical processes capable of preventing loss. It is an attempt to secure in the form of an external object, something he cannot secure internally: his own emotional core of being.

The compulsion to record expresses an elevated fear of the absence of, and possibly loss of, memory. The idea is that, by placing the memory outside (recording it), it will then be possible to find it in the way we find objects in the world outside: listening to and looking for them, just as we used our physical capacities to find our parents when we were young. This is what, in the developing child and in the adult, memory is for: a way to make the salient emotional experiences of our life available to us when we need them. Smith's effort here is to do so by recording moments in the lives of strangers.

Yet, the method Smith employs in its way assures that the memories will be lost in the chaos and clutter of too many recordings done without the kind of editing the mind applies when it selects what will and what will not become a memory. The compulsive way in which Smith seeks to do this with his photographs suggests the presence in him of a defect in his internal capacity to integrate life experience around a core of meaning. There is in Smith's compulsive need to make and save recordings of all kinds both a fear of loss and the expression of an impairment in the capacity to select, which is the capacity to know what memories matter. He fears he will lose memories because he has lost the capacity to know which ones matter, which is the capacity to attach the emotions to them that establish their significance. So, Smith is left with the question: Where in the chaos of remembered and imagined experiences and emotions can he find what is true and real? What appears to Smith as the failure of memory and the need to assist memory in holding on to what is vital in life, is, in reality, a failure to know what matters and what does not, which is the key to integrating experience around an emotional core. When we cannot know or find what matters, we find ourselves living a life in which nothing matters.

For the war correspondent, images of death, destruction, and darkness dominate. But it is not all you will find in Smith's work. In his photographs, you will find a wider range of emotion captured in the momentary, even fleeting, expressions of his subjects. This wide range of emotion is consistent with the idea that Smith's search is for emotion itself, that the emphasis on darkness tells us something about his secret: The range of emotions others have is what he has lost in himself. This is another way of speaking about the loss of home, the primary site where emotional life is meant to be nurtured.

As a war correspondent, Smith captured the horror of war: an unimaginable experience of death and destruction. He revealed the reality of war otherwise hidden by its distance from the people back home.

He brought the war home. After moving to his loft, Smith lives in a state not too far removed from squalor. His world is chaotic; there is no room for him to be with himself in it. There is, instead, a constant flow of visitors and a perpetual state of working on his life project. Thus, "home" is not a home if home is a place you can be with yourself. There are friends and visitors, but no family. There is a more or less permanently altered state of mind induced by drugs, alcohol, and cigarettes. He is both seeking an escape from his inner world and seeking, through his work, to find outside what he cannot locate within.

Inner freedom and memory

There is no freedom for Smith in his self-made world. In that world, he is a prisoner of his obsession. For Smith, unfreedom takes the form of the obsessive search for emotions in others and the creation of memories of those emotions by recording them in the form of photographs. In this, Smith resembles the replicants of *Blade Runner 2049* who also find their memories, and with them their emotional lives, in photographs of the families of strangers. Because these are the emotional lives of strangers and not his own, Smith cannot remember them. So, he pins them to his walls and spends his time searching them for clues to his emotional life. His obsessive need to take pictures stems from the absence of suitable memories and the emotional life they represent: unfreedom results from the unavailability of memories suitable to freedom.

Excessive commitment to external experiences is an important marker of a deficit in inner freedom. In this flight from freedom, work activities can play an important role, especially where those activities are taken on not by the necessity of making a living, but by the necessity of defending against the consequences of allowing oneself to have an internal experience. This is the deepest sense in which work life becomes a flight from freedom.

CHAPTER 7

Remembering and forgetting

Memory substitution

Familiar in psychoanalysis is the process of turning remembering into a form of forgetting, most notably when the memory we allow ourselves to have is meant not to connect us with the reality of our past but to prevent that connection from being made. This is accomplished by replacing the forbidden memory with one we find tolerable, even desirable. The result is memory substitution. Memory substitution is most notable in groups that come together for precisely that purpose. In the group, this means the construction of a group memory meant to occupy the space held by the memory of personal experience. The constructed past, then, sponsors an understanding of current-time emotional experience different from the understanding originally embedded in the salient experience.

Substitute memories may be of a happy past in which the group and its members thrived. But they may also be of freedom lost in the conquest of the group by hostile alien forces and the subjection, even enslavement, of group members. Then, the substitute past not only mirrors the repressed memory of a personal loss of freedom, but also replaces it as it transforms loss of freedom from a personal matter to a shared group experience. This substitution removes the experience from the inner world over which we feel we exert no control and transfers it into the external world where, paradoxically, control is thought to be possible through the magical power of the group, for example the power to enable its members to use others to contain the residue of their bad memories.

While memory substitution in groups is a natural extension of the original purpose of our memories, which is to represent a salient experience by taking a single event and making it represent a series of connected events and thereby invest meaning in our experiences, it can also serve the purpose of displacing the locus of that experience and fostering a misunderstanding of it. To consider the special opportunity afforded by memory substitution, we need to consider how the mind chooses the salient event not only to represent an emotion and help us manage relationships in the present and future, but also to attach a special kind of meaning to the chosen event. This special meaning involves forgetting salient aspects of the original event or events so that our feeling state may be reinterpreted especially with respect to the factor that provoked it. The importance in groups of what Vamık Volkan refers to as a "chosen trauma" (1988) lies in the way the group enables individuals to shift attention from the inner world, including the internalized form of past events, to events occurring long before members of the group were born.

Forgetting through substitution is another way of speaking about the processes of displacement and projection familiar in psychoanalysis. My concern here is with how to think about these processes in relation to both internal and external freedom, and to consider the question: What bearing does forgetting have on freedom? I will take as my example, one expression of the inheritance of slavery in the US: the call for reparations.

The inheritance of slavery

In testimony before the US House of Representatives, Ta-Nehisi Coates advocates the payment of reparations to the descendants of slaves in the US. He describes the purpose of reparations as gaining recognition for "our lineage as a generational trust, as inheritance, and the real dilemma posed by reparations is just that: a dilemma of inheritance.

It is impossible to imagine America without the inheritance of slavery" (2019). Coates' last comment deserves special attention. What he says, in effect, is that making reparation is about acknowledging the special importance of slavery, and, by extension, of the descendants of slavery, in America. It is about acknowledging that they matter. But, the notion of "inheritance" also merits special attention. That the problem to which Coates refers is a problem of inheritance draws our attention to the relationship between past and present and especially to the way the past is embedded in the present and therefore to the important role of memory.

Coates makes his case for reparations in an earlier article (2015). There, he begins with the following quote from the British philosopher John Locke (1690):

> Besides the crime which consists in violating the law, and varying from the right rule of reason, whereby a man so far becomes degenerate, and declares himself to quit the principles of human nature, and to be a noxious creature, there is commonly injury done to some person or other, and some other man receives damage by his transgression: in which case he who hath received any damage, has, besides the right of punishment common to him with other men, a particular right to seek reparation.

Coates begins, then, with the matter of law. This should alert us to the way he intends to understand damage and reparation, which is meant to be analogous to the way we understand crime and punishment. And, while existing statutes may not apply to past crimes for which reparation is meant to be paid, the legal model is still meant to be applied.

Damage has been done for which someone is responsible. The damaged party has the right not only to expect punishment for those responsible, but also to "seek reparation." Punishing the responsible party removes the onus for the harm from the victim, while paying reparations returns to the victim what has been taken from him. In a sense, both are efforts to make the damaged party whole, one with regard to self-worth, the other with regard to property and material well-being. The two are, of course, closely connected, as paying reparations is meant to be a restorative process for victims.

The damage to which Coates (2015) seeks to draw our attention began with slavery as did the benefits accruing to the white population: "Nearly one-fourth of all white Southerners owned slaves, and upon their backs the economic basis of America—and much of the Atlantic world—was erected. In the seven cotton states, one-third of all white income was derived from slavery."

This comment makes concrete the link between reparations and acknowledging that African Americans matter; that, without their contribution, something important would be missing, in this case something important in a tangible sense. The damage done to America's black population did not end with the end of slavery. Beyond the theft of black land, Coates notes in particular the consequences of discrimination in the housing market. He considers how, in Chicago, for example, whites employed measures ranging from restrictive covenants to bombings "to keep their neighborhoods segregated" (2019).

Coates emphasizes how the result of these measures designed to deprive blacks of the opportunity to own property was to create two separate worlds, one for whites the other for blacks. That deprivation was the end sought by those responsible could be seen in the result, which was that "average per capita income of Chicago's white neighborhoods is almost three times that of its black neighborhoods" (2019). The policies pursued by whites resulted in, and, according to Coates, were intended to result in, the creation of two different worlds.

Coates also highlights the history of the demand for restitution, referring to the way blacks who resisted measures designed to deprive them of their rights

> were charging society with a crime against their community. They wanted the crime publicly ruled as such. They wanted the crime's executors declared to be offensive to society. And they wanted restitution for the great injury brought upon them by said offenders. (2019)

Crimes that go unpunished have a special psychic resonance. When damage is done to an individual but not acknowledged, the reality of the damage is called into question and, with it, the recognition of the individual as someone who could be damaged, which is to say as someone who deserves to be treated with respect, is also cast in doubt. In the absence of punishment, the onus falls on the victim.

Coates uses this evidence to counter the idea that a policy of "affirmative action" could right the wrong done to black people. "Is affirmative action meant to increase diversity?" he asks. "If so, it only tangentially relates to the specific problems of black people—the problem of what America has taken from them over several centuries." In other words, affirmative action is aimed at improving the life prospects harmed by slavery and discrimination. But it is not meant to alter the *experience* of the past as that exists in the culture and psychology of the present.

Coates speaks both of material costs and costs in feelings of self-worth, noting, with regard to the latter, the message received by one young black boy from his country:

> You ain't shit. You not no good. The only thing you are worth is
> working for us. You will never own anything. You not going to get
> an education. We are sending your ass to the penitentiary.

He considers harms of this kind little affected by policies such as affirmative action. He also considers them the true harm to be addressed by reparations.

With regard to material costs, Coates quotes Yale Law professor Boris Bittker, who argued in *The Case for Black Reparations* (2003) "that a rough price tag for reparations could be determined by multiplying the number of African Americans in the population by the difference in white and black per capita income." The figure produced by this calculation was $34 billion in 1973 ($876 billion in current dollars). Coates acknowledges the practical limits to full reparation: "… after a serious discussion and debate … we may find that the country can never fully repay African Americans." But fully paying African Americans, if important in the abstract, is not the real purpose of reparations. Rather what is important about reparation is that, through the process of exploring the obligation to pay, "we stand to discover much about ourselves," a discovery "that is perhaps what scares us." Up to this point, Coates' emphasis has been on a quasi-legal interpretation of the problem: What has been taken must be restored. In this paragraph, however, a notable transition is made away from that construction of the problem. What is important is making a discovery, bringing something to light that has so far been hidden.

What is it that we stand to learn about "ourselves" and why does it scare us? "Reparations beckon us to reject the intoxication of hubris and see America as it is—the work of fallible humans." To connect the damage done to "fallible humans" makes the cause of damage personal and implies that someone must be made to feel responsible. Discussion of the wealth gap

> merely puts a number on something we feel but cannot say—that American prosperity was ill-gotten and selective in its distribution. What is needed is an airing of family secrets, a settling with old ghosts. What is needed is a healing of the American psyche and the banishment of white guilt.

Reparation is not simply about "recompense for past injustices." For Coates, reparation, or at least the discussion of it, is a "spiritual renewal" that "would mean a revolution of the American consciousness, a reconciling of our self-image as the great democratizer with the facts of our history." Reparations "would represent America's maturation out of the childhood myth of its innocence into a wisdom worthy of its founders." Reparation then, is about dispelling the image of the past carried forward into the present, which, to his way of thinking, constitutes a false memory.

What is clearest from Coates' account is that the past is not really in the past but remains alive in the present. The problem is what to do about this. And Coates' answer is that the past, as that is encoded in the psyches of black people, must somehow be instantiated in the minds of white people. What is important about the reparation discussion and process is that it will do this. Of course, it may not, so that expecting that it will may be a fantasy. White people may experience it not as a confrontation with their past, but as a puzzling annoyance or an act of aggression. Still, Coates hopes that reparations will establish a process that can finally move the past into the past.

In this, there is an idea of what people need and of what caring for those in need means. What black people need is relief from the burden of the past. This burden can be relieved only to the extent that their importance to the history of America can be acknowledged, and the burden of responsibility for their losses can be removed from them.

Their need, Coates insists, places an obligation of care on white people. This is an obligation couched in the language of justice.

Note how Coates uses the first person plural in speaking about the reparations process. By doing so, he points toward himself. Because of this, we may wonder if, in speaking the way he does, he acknowledges shared responsibility despite the fact that the demand for reparations is meant to designate an external locus of responsibility. Note also the reference to coming out of childhood. This suggests that, in some way, the discussion of reparations is a way of talking about childhood experience, indeed of his own childhood experience, of his history rewritten as the history of the nation. If it is, we can understand the reference to the growing awareness of the dark truth of our "spirit" as a growing awareness of the dark truth of his spirit transferred onto the nation, an effort simultaneously to confront and deny a personal reality. Note, finally, how acknowledging harm done and meeting the obligation it implies will relieve us of the stain on our soul, free us of our guilty conscience.

Reparations are meant to take bad feelings away from African Americans, relieving them of the conviction that there is a dark stain on their soul, that their plight is a punishment for their sins. After all, making restitution is a decision white America must *freely make*. It is a choice. It is a choice because white Americans can simply say no and there is no recourse if they do. White Americans can continue to see the plight of African Americans as their own doing, or, if not, as a result of a history which, as with all history, no one has the power to change: a situation that no living person caused or can affect and therefore for which no living person is responsible.

The problem is that this history lives on in the present as memory and fantasy. As an emotionally invested memory of the past it shapes the present and future. In this sense, the past exists in the present so that it is possible to change the past by altering memories, by forgetting at least in the sense of disinvesting memory of its meaning as a warning system relevant in the present. Coates hopes that memories can be disinvested (forgotten) in this way if the emotional investment in them can be moved outside, in this case onto white people. Doing so would, in effect, change the past as that exists in the present by changing our memories of it.

The call for reparations says: I want you to know how it feels to be punished for something you did not do, to be punished for who you are, and especially how it feels to accept an interpretation of the world and of yourself in which you deserve punishment even though you do not. This also points to the possibility that it is the internal situation of black people about which Coates speaks, and about himself. This would make his communication an effort to transfer a self-state of his own into another person, or in this case, a group of people.

Because of this, it is an act of aggression and provocation, and can best be understood by the target's response to aggression especially in the form of the defenses it provokes, including identification with the aggressor and the activation of the guilty self. The guilty self is a self that is driven to take responsibility for the bad things that happen to other people, for harm in which it may have played no part. All of this, then, makes caring about others mean taking a burden of guilt from them. Here, we come to one important meaning of obligation.

For Coates, obligation derives from guilt. Indeed, for him the two are so closely linked as to be indistinguishable. Guilt and responsibility can operate on two levels: the objective level of the assignment of responsibility on the basis of evidence and argument, and the subjective level of the experience of feeling guilty. Because reparations will not right a legally recognized wrong, Coates' line of argument depends on his ability to convince white people of their responsibility for the plight of black people and by so doing provoke in them the subjective experience of guilt. And, the only way this can work is if the members of his audience are already primed to take on responsibility for harm done by others, in other words are possessed of a guilty self.

Coates offers no reason to assume that his audience is configured in this way. This absence of evidence suggests that his assumption that they are comes not from an external source—evidence about the psychic lives of white people—but from an internal source: what he knows about himself and the way he knows it. In other words, this means that his argument for reparations is essentially driven by the hope to purge the guilty self from his inner world.

This much becomes clear if we recall Coates' insistence that what is important about reparations is the "airing of family secrets," the "settling with old ghosts." Speaking this way indicates that Coates considers the whole matter of reparations a family matter, and he considers white and black Americans members of a "family" in some important sense of the term. Thinking this way only makes sense if the demand for reparations expresses the incorporation of white people into roles in his personal family drama, in other words understands them as the incarnation in the world outside of internalized object relations. And, if this is what they are, they are also an expression of memory and of the power of memory.

Coates assumes that an account of the history of violence and exploitation will awaken in white people a sense of responsibility. They have not previously accepted their obligation because they were unaware of it. This absence of awareness can also be considered an intra-familial condition, the expression of something important about our relationship with those capable of determining whether we thrive or suffer. Once white people enter into a learning process (the discussion of reparation) they will no longer be able to ignore the facts of their history. They will learn what black people already know. Coates wants to educate someone about his suffering, someone who both causes and ignores it.

It needs to be emphasized that the solution proposed is one that continues a kind of dependency of blacks on whites. That Coates insists on continuing this dependency is clearly indicated in an alternative solution he rejects. This is the solution that finds that the plight of black America stems in part "from cultural pathologies that can be altered through individual grit and exceptionally good behavior" (Coates quoting Philadelphia Mayor Michael Nutter). According to Coates, this

> thread is as old as black politics itself. It is also wrong. The kind of trenchant racism to which black people have persistently been subjected can never be defeated by making its victims more respectable. The essence of American racism is disrespect.

Mayor Nutter's solution is for black people to adapt themselves to the external expectations of a society in which they are treated as second-class citizens. Coates will have none of this.

However we judge the specific solution offered by the idea of reparations, we should recognize that it is intended to move black people away from the demand that they adapt to white people's expectations about them. What it does not do is free them from their internalized expectations about being a black person, whether those expectations derive from white people or from their own families, though in Coates' formulation it is intended to do just that. Because it is intended to free black people from the guilt they feel for their condition and the suffering associated with feelings of guilt and the domination of the inner world by a guilty self, reparations, whatever their actual result would be, are intended to expand the inner freedom of black people precisely by freeing them of the need to adapt themselves to external expectations.

Reparations do so at the expense of the internal freedom of white people, who will now find their inner worlds tyrannized by the presence there of a guilty self. This trade-off exists because, in Coates' world, there is no escape from the guilty self, there is only a struggle over who will have it. Indeed, it is a struggle over whether all or only some will have it. And, because projecting guilt onto others does not purge the world of those suffering from their guilt, but only limits the degree of their suffering, the policy of reparations should be understood as a sharing of the guilty self rather than as a solution to the problem it poses.

This is the problem I have characterized in the language of obstacles to the free movement of thoughts and ideas. The presence of a guilty self in the inner world represents a fixed idea that is also the organizing principle for thinking and relating. The result of the presence of this fixed idea is a kind of stasis of the inner world due to the presence there of a force whose end is to assure adaptation to ideas about the self that block any effort to suspend presuppositions about who we are and what we wish to do in our lives. It alienates us from our own desires, which is to say desires rooted in the urge to give expression to our unique presence in the world.

The purpose of the guilty self is to redefine what we want no longer as gratification but as deprivation. For the guilty self, it is only by depriving ourselves that we can hold onto the hope that we will become worthy of gratification in the future. For the guilty self, this future cannot be in our lifetime because, so long as we remain alive, we must be preoccupied with suppression of our wants. The guilty self is the self merged with guilt, a self that exists in its repression. Because of this, guilt can never be overcome, or it cannot be overcome in our lifetime.

The purpose of discrimination and violent forms of oppression directed against groups is to provoke an identification with the oppressor that internalizes aggression against the self. This represents an attempt to transfer the self-hate of the aggressor onto his or her victim. Because it is an attack on the internal source of being and doing, internalization of the aggression against the self destroys internal freedom, which is its purpose. This then sets up an internal situation within the victim that mirrors that of the aggressor and defines what the victim needs: freedom from the internalized source of aggression. But the internal situation only allows one path to freedom: the transfer of the internalized source of aggression back to the aggressor or selected surrogates. But the solution via projection does not really purge the inner world of the attack on the self and create inner freedom. Rather, it becomes a permanent relationship with the aggressor and dependence on its continued presence.

Change

Coates begins by embedding reparations in a rights-based construction of the problems faced by African Americans. Property rightfully theirs has been taken from them. Reparations would return this lost property to its rightful owner. As his argument evolves, however, an alternative construction tends to displace the rights-based argument. This alternative also operates within a transactional understanding of the interpersonal world but shifts the issue on to an explicitly emotional plane. This is the plane of remorse and contrition. Placing the problems faced by African Americans on this plane is well expressed by the *Washington Post* columnist Jonathan Capehart (2019):

> At bottom, I bet you an apology is what African Americans want most. An acknowledgment of the pain and suffering, an expression of sorrow for the mistreatment and degradation, and an "I'm sorry" for the abasement of our ancestors and the disrespect (still) endured by their descendants. No check of any amount could substitute the priceless psychological benefit of a simple and sincere apology. Without one, our nation will never escape this endless loop of tragedy. We will never reconcile. We will never move forward.

Here, Capehart insists that a sincere apology, taken by itself, has the power to bring about a profound change. This clearly makes change something we can decide to do. More specifically, it calls on the ability of one individual to decide to bring about a desired change in the inner world of another. To put the matter in the language of the issue itself, this is the power to free the inner worlds of the ancestors of slaves, to replace a kind of inner enslavement with inner freedom. An apology will not alter the external oppression of African Americans: the absence of equal treatment in the criminal justice system, the contemporary consequences for them of discrimination in employment and home ownership, and so on.

To demand from someone that they return stolen property, secure your voting rights, or assure equal treatment before the law is to make demands about your external freedom. To ask or demand that they offer a sincere and "heartfelt" apology is to ask them to take responsibility for your inner freedom. Making this appeal assigns to those outside a role in the inner world. The slippage, evident in both Coates' and Capehart's accounts, between conceiving the issue as one of external and of internal freedom reflects the complex relationship between the two kinds of freedom. In part it expresses the wish or hope that securing external freedom will resolve the problem of unfreedom in the inner world. Like any expression of hope, it contains, more or less well hidden within it, doubt about the locus of the power to resolve a problem, especially doubt about the availability of the authority that has the power to do so.

Yet, while securing external freedom may be a necessary condition for securing internal freedom, it may not be a sufficient condition. This is because the hope expressed in the appeal to external authority denies its presence in the inner world. The underlying meaning of the appeal is the insistence that the external authority that imposes unfreedom as an external matter does not exist internally. This denial takes the form of projection of the authority outside onto a suitable container. Doing so makes the resolution of an internal problem a matter of will: the will of the external authority designated to have the power to relieve us of our emotional suffering. This construction is the essence of what I refer to as willful change, which is change conceived as the result of an act of will.

Part II

Concern for the welfare of others

CHAPTER 8

Concern for others

Adaptation and concern for others

In his book *Good Stuff*, Salman Akhtar explores what he refers to as "healthy, adaptive, and genuinely pleasurable aspects of human experience" (2013, p. xii), aspects he considers insufficiently studied by psychoanalysts. Under this heading, he includes experiences such as friendship, forgiveness, gratitude, generosity, and sacrifice, among others. All of these aspects of human experience are given the label "good," although that label is not itself subject to in-depth consideration. Still, it seems clear from the list of good stuff that good has two, possibly related connotations. First, it has to do with the nature and quality of the feeling state associated with experience of the good stuff. When we have a good-enough measure of the good stuff, we feel good. Second, good stuff has to do with connection. Good stuff connects people in a positive way. Friendship is a good thing; not having friends is bad. Forgiveness, generosity, and sacrifice all connect people in a "good" way. Of course, if connecting with others makes us feel good, then the two connotations will tend to merge. This is not, however, inevitably the case.

It appears that, at least in many cases, what is good about connection is that the presence in us of the good stuff is linked to our ability to get outside ourselves, to place a value on the well-being of others, even if that might diminish our own. If the good stuff creates a good feeling, then we feel good when we relate to others on a basis other than self-interest. Its complex relationship to self-interest suggests that the good stuff may not be related to good feelings in any simple or straightforward way. Generosity and sacrifice gratify us along one dimension while depriving us along another.

We can see this more clearly if we note how the good stuff is closely linked to what is morally good. As a moral category, good refers to doing things that elicit approval from others and especially from a group, indeed things that embed us in a group and subordinate us to it. Here, again, we are or do good because we sacrifice ourselves for something else, something larger and even transcendent. There is a connection, then, between the good stuff and what has long been thought of as the virtues needed to shape the character of the members of society if that society is to offer them a setting for a "good" life.

The importance of this aspect is clearly indicated by the inclusion of the adjective "adaptive" in the list of the "good" aspects of the human experience, at least insofar as membership in society means adapting to the values and norms that establish social order. Historically, culture and community are thought of as normative systems that can only sustain themselves so far as individuals adapt both in thought and conduct. But, as Winnicott points out (1986, p. 40), adaptation stands opposed to a central element in what feels good: creativity as expressed in the doing that expresses being. If the virtuous life is one of adaptation, then, by living it, we must suppress our urge to *exist*, to live in a way expressive of our original vitality or presence of being. If being able to make contact with the self is essential to well-being, and that is likely the case, then the attempt to identify the good with adaptation means that it will have a problematic relationship with well-being. Or, put another way, it will sustain the well-being of the group at the expense of that of the individual.

The question of adaptation is also important because it has a bearing on the matter of how real the virtue associated with the good stuff is, which is to say on the extent to which what we do is consistent with how we feel, whether the good stuff and the good feelings work together or tend to part company. When they part company, there is the potential for conflict between feeling good about ourselves and having the good stuff. This is not to say that we cannot feel good about ourselves when, for example, we are generous toward others. It does, however, suggest that we consider the difficult matter of how concern for others engages the self and whether it must do so in a repressive and hostile way. If the good does not feel good, is our living in a way consistent with it a genuine expression of who we are or an indication of the dominance in us of a false self? And what is the cost to us and to others if it is?

An important aspect of this potential conflict is the development of an opposition between the outward appearance of the self and what is real and true about it. Does having many friends indicate the presence of the good stuff or does it indicate a successful effort to appear as if we have the good stuff? The latter might be the case if, for example, we do not really enjoy spending time with our friends but feel protected from a harsh judgment of ourselves when they are around. This might also be the case in what Akhtar refers to as the "guilty intensification of gratitude" (2013, pp. 60–61), which, by linking gratitude to guilt, calls into question its goodness. Similarly, we may behave in a generous way when doing so gives us no pleasure and expresses not so much the presence of a generous character as a desperate need to be seen as generous, a need made more desperate by the certain knowledge, held in the recesses of the mind, that we are anything but generous. In other words, it indicates the presence of an ample supply of the bad stuff.

Akhtar's discussion makes it clear that we miss something important if we take it for granted that the good stuff is necessarily good, that it is always a good thing to express gratitude or engage in acts of generosity. We need to take seriously both the possibility that doing "good" things does not make us feel good and the further possibility that, to the extent that doing good means self-denial, it provokes exactly those feelings about which we are inclined to feel bad and that therefore have the potential to foster "bad" acts.

All of this bears directly on the matter of concern for others. The strength in the individual, and in the larger society, of concern for the well-being of others is often thought to indicate the presence of an abundant supply of the good stuff. In particular, it is often assumed that a stable social order depends on a deep and widespread concern for the well-being of others, even that social order is synonymous with concern for others because concern is the essential element in the social bond. This places considerable weight on the good stuff in assuring social cohesion.

The assumption that the good stuff, or concern for others, is, or should be, the essential element in the social bond is not inevitable or universally endorsed. It is not inevitable that a well-ordered society should be understood as one in which social cohesion depends on the suspension or even repression of self-interest. We should not take the role of the good stuff in the social bond for granted any more than we should take it for granted that the good stuff is good. In saying this, I do not mean to imply that it is my goal to establish that the good stuff is really bad, or that it is irrelevant to thinking about the factors that assure we do well living together. What I do think is that there are consequences to taking the issue as resolved before we engage in the process of thinking about it and that engaging in that process will lead to a better understanding of the matter and perhaps to some unexpected conclusions that reflect a more thoughtful approach to it.

To highlight the specificity of the use of the good stuff to underpin the kind of social bond that includes concern for others, I consider the good stuff in relation to the matter of entitlement. Are we entitled to well-being—do we have a right to welfare—or is our welfare our own responsibility? Does our right to welfare indicate the generosity of others and therefore the presence of the good stuff, or does it assure that we are not dependent on the virtue of others (the good stuff)? Is the good what is right or is an alternative that we consider the right what is good. I emphasize aspects of this question because the idea of rights immediately draws our attention to a sphere of individual self-determination, or, in the language used in Part I, freedom. Because of this, the difference between what is right and what is good suggests that the two can lead us in different directions with respect to the matter of concern for others. This difference can tell us something important about vital aspects of social connection and about the capacity of different kinds of social arrangements to provide the individual with space for self-determination in living.

How we acquire the things we need to secure our well-being is not independent of what we mean by well-being, of how we understand what the good stuff is. Whether we secure our welfare through the exercise of right or through, for example, the generosity of others is not just a matter of different paths to the same destination, it is also a matter of different destinations. And, those destinations differ not primarily in the obvious way—according to what things we get—but in less obvious ways having to do with the configuration of our inner worlds, which is ultimately where well-being resides and where we give shape to our goals in living.

Welfare

In exploring the psychodynamics of concern for others, I will take as an important case in point the matter of public support for welfare, and more specifically what it means to treat welfare provision as a matter of right. A formulation by David Frum (2016) challenges us to confront this issue: "Universal health coverage is not a human right, but in an advanced wealthy democracy, the lack of it is a great human wrong". In other words, it is morally wrong that some people do not have access to health care even though they may have no right to it. Can the good stuff play a role where a wrong exists that cannot be fixed by appeal to a right? The seeming paradox in this statement lies at the heart of controversy not only over matters of health care, but over many of the most powerful and divisive issues currently prominent in public debate.

Frum's comment resonated with me because I had spent a significant part of my career exploring how the idea of rights could be used to provide a basis for thinking about the welfare state. I pursued this line of thought because it seemed to me that failing to provide for needs such as those associated with health care was wrong in some sense, and therefore there must be something like a right not only to health care but to an important set of the things people need. My effort to argue that there exists a right to the things, or some of the things, people need, however, ran into some difficulties.

The idea that people have a right to things they need says something not only about the way they acquire what they need, but about *what* they need. This aspect of the problem is evident in the judgment about what sorts of things people have a right to acquire: health care, yes, a vacation home, no. Here, I bumped into an old question, or set of questions: What do people need? Should the set of things people need be distinguished from the set of things they want or desire, and does right extend only to things we need and not to those we "merely" want? After all, individuals may want a fulfilling personal life with friends and family, but it hardly seems plausible to argue for their right to have such a life even if they have the right to pursue it, at least within well-defined limits. Surely, we cannot simply assert that people have a right to things they need without knowing something about what people need and what sorts of needs we are talking about when we assert their right to have them met.

The question, what do people need, is a question about what sort of life they will lead and what sort of satisfaction they may expect to gain in living that life. The question about the existence of a "right" to the things we need leads us to ask about the appropriate way for individuals to go about acquiring the things they need and especially about the kind of dependence on others embedded in the activity of need satisfaction.

Attempting to answer the first question leads us to consider such matters as the extent to which what we need is a personal matter related to what is unique about us—our individual identity, self-determination, our "being" in Winnicott's sense of the term. It also leads us to consider, as an alternative to needs linked to what is distinct about us, needs linked to our group identity and likely therefore to promote adaptation of the self to the demands of group life, especially a greater or lesser degree of submergence of identity into the group and the loss of self implied by it. The answer to the second question, then, depends on the answer to the first, though not in any simple or straightforward way. Complexity arises for a number of reasons but one of the most important is an ambiguity about the term "right." On one side, right is a term we associate with the freedom to choose and through choosing to establish a way of life expressive of our unique presence of being. On the other side, the term has come to mean the kind of entitlement to a common way of life through the equal satisfaction of needs present in all of us. The most notable, but not the only, example of this second way of using the term is for access to health care.

When Frum insists that, while there is no right to health care, it is wrong to deprive people of it, he offers a judgment about the activity or process of need satisfaction. By taking the satisfaction of need outside the sphere of right, he would seem to move it onto a terrain on which whether needs get satisfied, most notably by those lacking the financial resources to acquire them for themselves, depends on two related factors: (1) the charitable sentiments of the larger community, and, in a democratic society, (2) the extent to which the majority feel there is something wrong about not providing health care to those who cannot afford it. This suggests that the heart of the matter is whether provision of health care, for example, will be made to depend on the moral sentiments prevailing in the community, which would make health care contingent in a way the language of right does not. It would depend on how many citizens agree with Frum that it would be wrong to deny health care to anyone because they cannot afford it.

Of course, this distinction may be less real than it at first appears to be. After all, in a democratic society, rights are, at least to a significant degree, contingent on the sentiment of the electorate. As it turns out, even those who insist on a right to health care, and perhaps other things people need, tend not to offer any reasons that might convince others not already committed to the idea, but rather use the term right not as a summary of reasons but as a way of investing their preferred policy with a special emotive power. Clearly, once a program is put in place that assures universal access to health care independently of the ability to pay, we can speak of the result as a "right" to health care, but that would hardly constitute an argument in favor of universal health care before it has been made a reality. It could not be used to convince someone who is not already convinced.

There is a sense in which the point about rights is that they are to be respected even if they are not favored by the majority. In other words, the use of the language of right is intended to protect the individual from decisions made by the group. Then, the implicit argument for a right to health care is that health care for the individual should not be made contingent on the sentiment of the group. Yet, the use of the language of right and the emotional charge invested in it does not protect access to health care if it is not part of the sentiment of the group that those who cannot afford care ought nonetheless to have it. This means that however we may seek to protect the "right" to health care from the sentiment of the group, we cannot avoid dealing with the issue. Does the health care of those who cannot afford it matter to us, and if so why? Is it important that the welfare of others matters to us? Can a robust welfare state develop where the welfare of others does not matter to us?

Of course, it is not sentiment in general that is involved in the issue of why people are or are not drawn to the idea of assuring the welfare of others. It is the specific sentiment that in some sense makes each of us invested in the welfare of others. So, when we consider the matter of sentiment in relation to taking responsibility for the well-being of others, we are necessarily considering the matter of the nature and meaning of social connection. There are, after all, sentiments that drive us apart and lead us either not to care what happens to other people or possibly to find gratification in the harm that comes to them.

Concern for the well-being of others is often taken for granted as an inborn impulse expressed most notably in the sentiment we refer to as compassion. Problems arise because compassion is bound up with identification, which makes concern for others an aspect of our concern for ourselves. It also requires that we dismiss salient differences between self and other. Indeed, a common problem in reliance on sentiment to account for concern for others is that it tends to distort what others need by investing too much of our own need in the act of providing care for them. This can mean that our concern for others is not what it seems to be, that it is not really concern for *their* welfare but a complex expression of concern for our own. If this is the case, then we need to consider more closely the matter of concern for others to see how the different roots of concern shape relating, and, for this, we need to consider concern for others not a simple expression of a human urge to care, but a more complex expression of an underlying emotional configuration. In doing so, it will prove useful to turn to psychoanalysis, which is specifically concerned with the forces that shape our emotional experience of self and other.

Psychoanalysis has identified a number of emotional drivers that affect not only our capacity for concern, but also what being concerned for the welfare of others means to us, including: identification, guilt, the reparative impulse linked to guilt, gratitude, and generosity. I have elsewhere considered guilt and reparation at some length (Levine & Bowker, 2019) and will not repeat those discussions here. In this study, my focus will be on the possibility of looking to the good stuff in our attempt to identify the foundation for the kind of concern for others that sustains social-cultural systems.

CHAPTER 9

Gratitude

Transactional relations

Consider the following comment on the virtues underpinning a democratic society offered by Michael Gerson (2018):

> Democracy is not merely a set of procedures. It has a moral structure. The values we celebrate or stigmatize eventually influence the character of our people and polity. Democracy does not insist on perfect virtue from its leaders. But there is a set of values that lends authority to power: empathy, honesty, integrity, and self-restraint. And the legitimation of cruelty, prejudice, falsehood, and corruption is the kind of thing, one would think, that religious people were born to oppose, not bless.... At its best, faith is the overflow of gratitude, the attempt to live as if we are loved, the fragile hope for something better on the other side of pain and death. And this feather of grace weighs more in the balance than any political gain.

If we consider Gerson's comment an attempt to understand what makes our life together possible, what power we can set against the destructive forces, most notably of hate and greed, that pull us apart, his answer is gratitude. And taken in this way, Gerson's comment can be considered a counterpoint to Freud's insistence that it is guilt that holds us together against the forces that would divide us.

Gratitude holds us together because of its connection to love, which is the original binding force. Gratitude is sometimes understood as the word we use to refer to our response to being loved. In other words, gratitude is our response to an object that provides gratification. Perhaps paradoxically, gratitude is what we offer in return for gratification provided without any expectation of a return. Expressions of gratitude offer gratification to those who have provided us with good feelings, a sense of security in ourselves, a sense of being cared about.

It may seem odd, however, that, in speaking of gratitude, Gerson highlights the idea of living "*as if* we are loved" (emphasis added). Doing so makes the gratitude he emphasizes different from gratitude as that is usually understood, which is a feeling provoked when love has been received, not a response to love imagined in its absence. Considered in this way, gratitude either exists or it does not, depending on whether there was or was not love. Melanie Klein refers to gratitude understood in this way when she sees in it an important basis for securing the social bond. For Klein, gratitude has its origin in the early provision of a secure and nurturing environment. It is the child's emotional response to the provision of care; it is an aspect or expression of love. The early experience of being cared for is then transferred onto adult relationships. As she puts it, gratitude "becomes the foundation for devotion to people, values, and causes" (1957, p. 187). In drawing this conclusion, she seems in line with Gerson's emphasis on gratitude although the gratitude she highlights lacks the as-if quality Gerson attaches to it.

Yet, there is only gratitude where, in Winnicott's language, the infantile illusion of the ability to create the world does not define the whole of the relationship with a maternal object. Under the sway of this illusion, the infant considers gratification an aspect of need, something automatically brought into being by need itself. Where the infantile illusion dominates, the infant feels a kind of entitlement, although that term does not yet apply. Because one does not feel grateful for receiving something to which one is entitled, feeling entitled gets in the way of gratitude. This casts doubt on the idea that gratitude originates in the early maternal connection emphasized by Klein (see Akhtar, 2013, p. 58).

If we do not feel entitled to love, then it only comes to us at a price; there must be an implicit quid pro quo. We must, for example, do something to deserve it. All of this tends to make parenting a transactional relationship, which then leads to seeing adult relationships also as transactions. To make the matter more concrete, consider the following example.

> George was the manager of a division within a larger organization. As head of the division, he had a pool of money to be used at his discretion. He also determined the allocation of funds for annual salary increases. George used these funds to reinforce his position in the minds of his employees as the person who could adjudicate their well-being by providing or withholding funds they might use, for example, to take trips to conferences, for professional development, or for salary enhancement. Making money available was also a way of securing friendships with favored employees. Indeed, being one of George's friends was a precondition for surviving in the organization as those who were not his friends tended to become pariahs, whose salaries stagnated and who were passed over for the more desirable assignments.
>
> The allocation of benefits in the division was meant to secure the idea that George was a generous person, although by other measures he was not. None of the money George spent on his favored employees came out of his own pocket. He never offered to pay for a meal. So, his largesse never cost him anything. And, indeed, by other measures, George was willing to share very little with others who always knew, for example, that the decision-making authority in the division was closely held by George, that prestige, regard, and power were never shared but always used to feed George's greedy narcissism. One result of this was that greedy narcissism became a hallmark of the division as employees found themselves in a struggle for whatever measure of the good things remained after George claimed his own. The division was a vehicle George used to establish his generosity while hiding the fact that his primary motive was feeding his endless need for the

greatest possible measure of the good things, and always more than anyone else could have.

For George, gratitude was a one-way street. It was important that his employees felt gratitude toward him, that they never lost sight of the source of the good things they received. But George was never grateful for the simple reason that the only thing he wanted from employees was their gratitude, for which he did not feel grateful but entitled. The friendship he purchased from them and the recognition of his exceptional qualities as an administrator were things for which he assumed they ought to be grateful.

One could say that what George was looking for was a surrogate for love in the admiration for his qualities and gratitude for his pseudo-generosity. But, because the employees paid a considerable price to be the recipients of George's pseudo-generosity, nowhere in the organization was there much room for real gratitude and real generosity. If the experience of this relationship could be considered a way George sought to transfer onto employees his own experience of love or the lack thereof, to communicate what he received as a child and what he did not, then we can conclude that George did, indeed, experience a deficit in what Michael Balint refers to as "primary love" (see below), and that this experience defined what generosity meant to him. It meant that to be generous is to impose a fantasy of himself as a generous person on those over whom he had the power to do so, and, indeed, to get them to see in his greedy narcissism proof of his generosity. His goal was to enforce the substitution of his fantasy for reality by assuring that everyone in the division acted *as if* it were real.

George's way of relating was essentially transactional, and he considered gratitude squarely within his transactional construction of the world. Gratitude contains this transactional element insofar as we consider it payment of an emotional debt. The expectation of payment moves gratification outside the terms set by primary love. Only when the source of our gratification is seen to provide it at his or her will (by choice) can real gratitude be provoked. This means that the more the source of gratification expects and insists on gratitude, the less is real gratitude provoked.

As Akhtar (2013) points out, our motivation to offer expressions of gratitude in return for gratification provided may vary depending on a number of factors. Most important for our purposes is the extent to which the expectation of gratitude was a significant part of the offer of gratification and whether the recipient feels that expressing gratitude will undermine his or her positive investment in the self, in other words whether being grateful provides evidence of a form of dependence that undermines the sense of having a secure and reliable internal capacity to care for the self. This connects with the move toward an overtly transactional experience of gratification, which can also be felt to undermine the individual's positive emotional investment in the self.

The entry point for the transactional view of relating can be found in an important quality of parenting. Central to the parent–child relationship is the ability of the parent to carry an emotional burden for the child and to do so in a way that is not reciprocated. Especially in the early stages of life, the emotional burden was literally the burden of the difficult emotions experienced by the child. That is, the parent actually took on those emotions by accepting the child's efforts to transmit them via the method of projective identification. Having taken on the child's emotion, the parent then managed it internally and returned it to the child in a form that could be tolerated, especially by moderating the emotion so that the experience of it became survivable. In this sense, managing emotions could be considered a kind of transaction.

This whole situation fosters a transactional construction of relating, however, only to the degree that the parent conveys to the child that a debt has been created, that the care provided has cost the parent something, and that the child is responsible for imposing that cost. If this message has been conveyed, there will be established in the child the idea that benefits received mean a debt incurred so that life will be experienced as a system of transactions patterned on the primary transaction, which is the one in which care and love were treated as currency.

This idea can become a norm, adherence to which assures that the culturally embedded understanding shapes the family dynamic. When this happens, the use of gratitude in the way depicted in our example indicates the transmission into adult life of forms of greed linked to early experiences of deprivation. In other words, the construction of care as imposing a burden and creating a debt is a response to the parent's experience, conveyed to the child, of neediness as a form of greed that damages the only available source of gratification. The idea conveyed by the parent that gratification depletes its source makes gratification and deprivation two sides of one phenomenon with the most significant consequences for the way we understand what it means to be concerned with the welfare of others. Along these lines, Winnicott notes that "most gratitude, certainly exaggerated gratitude, is a matter of propitiation; there are avenging forces latent, and they had better be appeased" (1986, p. 118; see also 1960, p. 149). In our language, the stronger the trans-actional component of the relationship the more marked the move-ment in the direction of pseudo-gratitude. If there is a healthy form of gratitude, it arises out of the kind of internal source of security in the self that develops when primary love is not impaired by the expectation of a return.

We can better understand the connection between caring about others and early experiences of care if we consider what Michael Balint refers to as "primary love," the demand for which tends to equate love with being loved, and indicates, when dominant in the adult, a failed transition in the direction of a love that is shared and reciprocated. To receive primary love is to "be loved and looked after in every respect by everyone and everything important to me, without anyone demanding any effort or claiming any return for this." For the recipient of primary love, only their "own wishes, interests, and needs" matter. Others must subordinate their wishes and needs "without any resentment or strain" (1969, pp. 70–71).

When primary love has not been impaired, the conditions are put in place for the internalization of the good object and the relationship with it. Internalization of the good-object relationship establishes the capacity to care for the self, which then makes it possible to receive good things from others for which we express gratitude because being depen-dent on others does not activate the problematic feelings associated with an object relationship in which love was never freely given, and the feel-ing of being loved never fully established as a reality of the inner world.

When driven by the need to elicit gratitude, what appears as care about the welfare of others is, in reality, an attempt to defend the self against awareness of significant deficits in the care received early in life. Demanding gratitude of the child requires that the child convince herself that she has gotten something for which to feel grateful and that she should live *as if* that were the case. The need served in relating to others is to comply with their insistence that deprivation is a form of care. And, because there is a level of the psyche, however hidden from our awareness, on which we know that deprivation is not care, our gratitude contains a significant element of resentment. This, then, is the starting point for grievance.

Gratitude expressed as generosity is the sentiment meant to promote concern for the welfare of others. The desire to make gratitude an aspect of the provision of welfare is also a desire to make that provision a relationship in which love plays a part. But the resentment embedded in gratitude can make it a problematic basis for the social bond in general, and for the possibility that care about the welfare of others would be part of that bond.

Primary love

While it may seem counterintuitive, impairment in the ability to be concerned about the welfare of others develops not out of an excess of primary love, but out of a deficiency in it. A deficiency in primary love impedes the development of an internalized experience of being cared for. Internalization makes it possible for the experience of care to exist in the absence of the primary object who provided care without making any demands of his or her own. It is important to bear this in mind because it is often assumed that providing primary love encourages greed and, because of that, gets in the way of the development of generosity. However, because primary love can be considered the feeding of a primitive form of greed, it allows internalization of the object that fed us and of our relationship with that object. This feeding of primitive greed, then, sets a foundation for generosity in adult life.

If gratitude has a root in being cared for, it also has a root in the failure to be cared for. Indeed, the term "gratitude" contains the possibility of failure because implied in it is the condition that our power over the source of gratification is not absolute but conditional. This is another expression of the point made earlier that we do not feel gratitude for receiving something to which we feel entitled, which is implicitly a need the satisfaction of which we feel we can control. To feel entitled is to deny the separation of the source of gratification from our will, which is tantamount to denying that the source of gratification has a will of its own and therefore can withhold gratification. Similarly, entitlement, or right, has an absolute quality and demands to be recognized independently of the will of those responsible for assuring that needs are met. Unconditional gratification stands opposed to the gratification for which gratitude is demanded or even expected.

Internalization of the capacity for primary love makes more mature forms of love possible and therefore sets the basis for reciprocity in caring. By making care an internal object relation, the individual establishes a degree of independence from it and thereby invests care with a degree of contingency on the continuation of the feeling toward the other that establishes him or her as an instantiation in the world outside of a remembered experience. If the other person is not established as a part of our inner world in this way, gratitude does not develop. This contingency of gratitude limits its capacity to operate as a motivating factor in general and limits its operation to those with whom we have established a connection of a particular kind.

Internalization makes it possible for us to relate to others according to the pattern established in our relationship with a good object, which is an object that provided reliable attention to and satisfaction of our needs. The result of the internalization of a good object is that "in making sacrifices for somebody we love and in identifying ourselves with the loved person, we play the part of a good parent, and behave towards this person as we felt at times the parents did to us—or as we wanted them to do" (Klein, 1992, pp. 311–312).

Concern for the well-being of others is a capacity born of an early connection with an object that assures our needs will be satisfied. This is a connection in which love and need satisfaction are, or ought to be, inseparable, especially if we consider need's object not in a purely material sense, but as the nutrients that sustain emotional life. These nutrients, because of their provision in the act of need satisfaction in the material sense, come to represent emotional sustenance. Satisfying material needs is, of course, important in itself, but it is also important as an expression of an emotional connection that satisfies our emotional needs: to feel cared for and therefore safe in the communication of our emotional need, to feel assured that the communication of need will be received and responded to.

The point can be highlighted by an example from a class I taught on the welfare state. During one session I asked the students whether they favored right or charity as the way of securing welfare for those unable to do so on their own. The clear majority of students favored charity. When asked why, they responded that it was better to receive care from those who care rather than those who don't. In other words, they preferred to make care part of a personal rather than impersonal connection. Embedded in this preference was the desire to assure that a measure of love was attached to care, suggesting that it is also love we seek when we need the care of others. The way my students thought about welfare provision made it contingent on the presence of love. Unless we love everybody, something which is, as Freud emphasizes, inconsistent with the idea of love, making welfare provision contingent on love puts it at considerable risk. What my students did not take into account is that once we move others into the world of emotional salience, having them matter to us may mean loving them, but it may also mean hating them.

In particular, strangers do not fit the criteria that must be met by someone we love since by definition we can only love those we know, which is to say those we relate to as instantiations of internalized object relations within which we were cared for. In other words, it makes care a form of knowing and this creates difficulty if we come to depend on strangers for our care as is often, if not inevitably, the case. If internaliza-tion of a caring relationship is to shape the social bond, we must relate to strangers as if they are family members because, emotionally, that is what we make them. The problem that arises here is that this outside world is not our family, which means that we will misunderstand it if we assume, however unconsciously, that it is. Strangers are not family. They do not and have not loved us, and we have no reason to be grateful to them, or they to us. To the extent that this is the case, the power of the as-if world tends to weaken the more we allow ourselves to acknowledge that reality differs from it.

Taking control and right

Early in life, when our needs were not satisfied, we did not feel loved. This experience becomes, later in life, the conviction that our inability to satisfy our needs confirms that we are unworthy of love, which means that we suffer deprivation in the most basic sense of the term. In our effort to cope with this situation, movement into the as-if world can play an important part. The as-if world is one in which we were loved, which is to say our needs were satisfied. Thus, Gerson's answer to the question, what does it mean to feel gratitude for love not received, would seem to be that gratitude is an expression of a fantasy. Even if we were not loved, we can come to believe that we were. Then, we can feel gratitude for the love we believe we received. It is, after all, in the nature of belief that we deploy its power against reality.

A further advantage of the as-if or believed-in world is that it makes need satisfaction something over which we can, albeit in fantasy, exert control. We may not be able to make our caregivers love us, but we can make ourselves believe that they do (or once did). This effort on our part to take control of what we believe facilitates the effort on the part of others to do so as well. In the as-if world, taking control means telling people how they feel, or ought to feel, and raises the question: Is it necessary, or even helpful, to tell people how they should feel, or how they need to feel, if we are to sustain a larger world of relating to others in the face of aggression and self-interest? After all, in no small measure, the power of the as-if argument depends on the assumption that we can decide how to feel about ourselves and others based on how we *should* feel, which also makes it possible for others to influence how we feel so far as they can exert a measure of control over our decision about how we should feel. Does our effort to move into the as-if world work? Do we come to feel love and gratitude based on a fantasy relationship that may be, for many people, the opposite of the one they really had?

The attempt to take control through giving instruction is part of a larger trend in public life that involves telling people what emotions they have the right to feel. This trend has roots in the intensely held wish that we can overcome our situation and the frustrations and anxieties associated with it by an act of will. Control over others, then, is a strategy for asserting control over our experience of ourselves projected onto others. At the same time, it makes others responsible for the way we feel, and, to this degree, we can take willful control over our own emotional experience by taking control over theirs. This means projecting onto them our feelings of having our selves controlled from outside. This system of emotional interrelating can then be experienced through the

prism of right, as it is when we attempt to assert ourselves as the adjudi-
cators of who has a right to feel the way they do.

Thus, distinctions are drawn between those who have a right to feel
victimized and those who do not, between those who have a right to feel
angry and those who do not, between hate that is justified and hate that
is not. When we speak of our right to be angry or aggrieved, we insist
that our feelings are in some important sense *real* while the feelings of
others are not. This special reality of some feelings is often linked to
deprivation so that it is deprivation that creates right. This clearly has
important emotional roots in early relationships in which needs were
not satisfied so that right is used in the sense of making something right
that had gone wrong. Then, insistence on the right to the things we need
follows from the legitimacy of our grievance about our deprivation.
But, in our reexperience of the primitive relationship later in life, the
feeling of deprivation only comes into play because of the failure of an
original entitlement. Without that element, we may still make a claim
to assistance in acquiring the things we need, but that claim would not
rest so securely on the idea of right. Or, put another way, in our minds
the ideas of right and grievance (deprivation) have become inseparably
linked in the way Coates links them in his discussion of reparations.

The gratitude felt for love we did not receive may be, at least in one
important sense, false, but this makes it no less important to those who
experience it. Indeed, they may embrace it not simply because others
tell them to, but because doing so is felt to be vitally important to their
emotional equilibrium, even to their emotional survival. If this happens,
then the strategy embodied in the effort to tell people how they should
feel can work, at least up to a point. To be more precise, what it can do is
set in motion an internal struggle, ongoing mainly outside of awareness,
between opposed feelings: those we have about other people and those
we are meant to have.

This struggle becomes well established when embracing gratitude
operates as a defense against the emotional consequences of acknowledging that we were not loved, or that we were not loved enough. Then
the external insistence that we ought to feel in a certain way combines
forces with an internal imperative. A deficit in love fosters the conviction
that we are unworthy of love. It is this possibility that gratitude protects
us against. So, we convince ourselves that we are grateful, because only

by doing so can we convince ourselves that we have something to be grateful for. We are wealthy where it matters, and others are poor. So far as this conviction is widespread, it can, as Gerson suggests, play a large role in shaping the social bond, one aspect of which is that it represents the presence of love so that our involvement in it indicates that we have those qualities of personality that make us worthy of love.

Yet, deprivation, before it promotes gratitude, promotes aggression against those we hold responsible for the care we have not received. If we come to see in our aggression the major obstacle to gratification, we may turn to gratitude as a defense against the emotional consequences of the thought that our destructive impulse is responsible for our deprivation. Keeping this impulse in check keeps hope alive by preventing us from damaging the object whose love we hope to gain. Where gratitude prevails, we should also expect to find forms of pseudo-generosity.

Love and dependence

People may have different ideas about what it means to care for others, but the most deeply rooted of these ideas are embedded in the internal relationship rather than expressed in their explicitly articulated statements. When we refer to them as caring or uncaring, we typically refer to our interpretation of their actions, which is, in turn, shaped by the reality of our inner worlds and not by any separately determined reality of their lives.

Consider, as an example, the following interchange I once had with a student. This interchange occurred immediately after a class session on the subject of tolerance, which came at the end of a course on the subject of hatred and group conflict. In the session, we explored the idea that tolerance may play an important role as the alternative to hate. In response to this, the student told me that he felt tolerance was too small a thing, too weak a force to act as a counterweight to hate. Something more was needed; and, in his view, this something more was not to tolerate difference but to *value* those who are different, indeed, to value them for what is different about them. This is how he, implicitly at least, understood what the nature of the social bond ought to be.

In response, I suggested to the student that tolerance was no small thing. Rather, it was a considerable and difficult achievement to be able to live peacefully with those to whom we feel indifferent at best, to give up belief that we are loved and to be all right doing so, to live in a world outside the confines of the place of familial connection, which is the place where our connections with others are based on our love for them and their love for us. In effect, I was telling him that his way of conceiving the social bond expected too much and too little: too much care for and interest in the individual, and too little respect for the boundaries that separate people and protect them from being absorbed into the fantasy worlds of others.

What this student seemed to be seeking in the larger world of social relating is a form of love patterned on early childhood experience. And, the fact that he remained dissatisfied with anything less, or anything different, suggests that a not fully satisfied need for primary love left him with a continuing sense that something was missing in his life and that this something was to be sought in settings where it is hardly likely to be found. Indeed, when we consider many settings of adult welfare provision outside the family, we can hardly avoid this link to early deficits.

The problem can be formulated in the following way. The inability of individuals to care for themselves or to find the needed care in their family fosters a seeking after care outside the setting where love is available as a vital aspect of care. At the same time, seeking love outside the family creates a kind of dependence that diminishes self-esteem and identifies the individual as unprepared emotionally to live independently as an adult in an adult world. Additionally, seeking love outside the family can mean seeking a repetition of an early experience of frustration, which is now inseparably linked to seeking love so that seeking love has come to mean seeking an experience of deprivation of love. As a result, at the same time that a form of primitive love is sought, the need for it must also be denied. Thus, the problematic demand for relationships shaped by the need for primary love but couched in a language designed to hide that need, for example the demand for admiration or the use of the language or right to characterize the provision of things meant to satisfy need.

Right attaches need satisfaction to entitlement, thereby replacing the weakness of dependence with strength. On one side, the term "right" recalls a vital aspect of the primitive relationship through which needs are satisfied on demand, and in a way that prompted Winnicott to speak about the way the maternal connection can foster in the infant an illusion of omnipotence. At the same time, the term right, when invoked in the adult setting, is meant to dismiss the relational element in need satisfaction and the element of dependence implied in it. Right assumes that we are entitled to receive a benefit from those who are not in a relationship of familial obligation.

This tension would not seem to arise for those who reject the idea that there is a right to welfare. Yet, however the rejection of this right may seem opposed to insistence on it, rejection of rights' claims can also carry indications of their origin in primitive emotional experience. Thus, the assumption that there can be no right to the things we need may reflect denial of the presence in adult life of any residue of the more primitive forms of dependence, notwithstanding the inevitability that such a residue exists and retains a greater or lesser power over adult experience. If this denial is rooted in the equation of love with deprivation referred to above, it will not be surprising to find a significant element of aggression, even hate, mixed into the movement against the provision of welfare for those in need. This suggests the possibility of a basic inconsistency between use of the language of right and the rooting of the social bond in gratitude, and therefore implicitly in love. The latter calls upon the terms of a relationship defined by intimacy and attachment in a world where what is important is what is special about us. Right puts all that aside in favor of a connection to what is claimed to be universal in us.

CHAPTER 10

Generosity

Generosity and self-interest

When you have a right, you do not depend on anyone's generosity. But it may be that, if your intent is to create a right, to do so you will need to call on generosity or somehow deal with the absence of generosity. Thus, in the movement to institute universal access to health care in the US, those who advocate making health care a right find themselves avoiding any implication that extending equal access to all will adversely affect those already having coverage. They do so by insisting that there will be no additional cost to a massive expansion of coverage either because the additional costs will be fully covered by gains through greater efficiency or because whatever additional costs remain after efficiency gains will be fully covered by a new tax that falls entirely on the wealthiest part of the population. No mention is made of the stress placed on medical services by the added coverage, for example in the form of longer waiting periods.

Recourse to these arguments (or in the latter case to silence on an important issue) can be taken to indicate that advocates of a right to health care are less than confident that they can expect the generosity of the electorate to secure support for their programs. To be sure, polling indicates that a substantial majority of voters favor universal coverage. But, as with many similar measures intended to set a floor on living standards, there remains a significant gap between support for programs in principle and willingness to pay for them. In other words, it indicates the presence of significant doubt about the likelihood of success in creating a right that has a significant cost associated with it if doing so is made to depend on generosity.

If you cannot rely on generosity, can you rely on people acting as if they were generous? If we can provide a right to health care with no cost to those who already have access, then we can act as if we are generous by speaking and voting for the expansion of access to affordable care. And if doing so creates a right, or something equivalent to it, then that right, once in place, protects the individual's access to care from the danger otherwise posed to it by the absence of generosity, or the absence of a sufficient measure of generosity, to support care for those who need it but cannot afford it.

Should we consider this deficiency in generosity a defect in the moral standing of the nation, something that can perhaps be rectified by better education in the value system that underpins democracy and citizenship? It can be argued, after all, that so long as generosity remains of the as-if variety, no rights, especially in the area of welfare, can ever be secure. Thus, subsequent to passage, the Affordable Care Act came under significant and nearly successful attack by the subsequent administration. The slogan that most successfully undermined the Act was "repeal and replace with a better and less costly plan."

The argument against it relied heavily on the presence in the Act of a provision to tax workers who chose not to purchase care. One of the provisions that saved the Act was the one that made it illegal for insurance companies to refuse care on the basis of preexisting conditions, a provision favored by the electorate not out of generosity but self-interest. Security of the Act can be said to depend on either self-interest or an as-if variety of generosity that is a thinly veiled version of self-interest. Is a better system of education in the values including generosity an alternative or simply another thinly veiled version of a self-interest that indicates the absence of generosity and protects the community from the destructive forces of self-interest by marshalling a kind of pseudo-generosity to hide it? To answer this question, we need a better understanding of the virtues that sustain care for others and also a better understanding of the meaning and implications of behaving as if we were generous when we are not.

* * *

What, exactly, is generosity? Consider first the following definition from the University of Notre Dame: Generosity is "the virtue of giving good things to others freely and abundantly" (2019). This brief definition tells us several important things about generosity. First, generosity is a virtue. In other words, it is a good thing, and it is a good thing that resides in the character of the individual (or fails to); it is a quality of his or her being. Second, generosity is the quality of the individual expressed in an act, or series of acts, of a special kind. These are the acts by which the individual gives good things to others, and does so "freely," in other words without the expectation of a return. This means that, unlike gratitude, generosity is not essentially transactional. Finally, this giving of the good things to others is no small matter, no transfer of an amount of the good things that makes little difference. Rather, it is the transfer of the good things "abundantly."

Implicit in this is the idea that the good things transferred are good not only to the recipient, but also to the one who gives them. If I give a good thing to you that is no good to me, then the act hardly rises to the standard set by generosity. If I have a billion dollars and give you one, that is hardly generous. In fact, it suggests the opposite of generosity. It could even be said, contrary to the habit in transactions between the wealthy and charitable institutions, that if I have a billion dollars and give a million to charity, this does not indicate that I possess or exhibit the virtue of generosity. For generosity, something more is needed. Furthermore, it is not generosity if, in the act of providing you the good things, I also convey a sense that doing so is costly to me and therefore you should be grateful for my generosity. There is no generosity where giving entails a demand for gratitude as payment.

In spite of the implication of the definition offered above, generosity is sometimes thought of in transactional terms, as is the case, for example, in the following comment from Tchiki Davis on the subject: "Generosity is a good thing for *our mental health and well-being* because when we give to someone we care about, we make it more likely for them to give to us, making us more likely to give to them, and so on" (Davis, n.d.). While this hardly seems in the spirit of the idea of generosity, it does raise a useful question: What drives generosity? Why be generous?

One possible answer is that we engage in generous acts because generosity is judged to be a virtue and we crave recognition of our virtue, which is our identification with the good. But, if this is the case, in what sense is our act virtuous? Indeed, in what sense is it a generous act, given that it is a way for us to lay claim to the good and not an act by which we freely give to others? Is an individual who cares nothing about art or about public access to it but donates money to an art museum because of a desire to have his or her name attached to the museum a generous person? More generally, if giving is done with the purpose of gaining recognition for being good is it a generous act or an act of self-aggrandizement? Does it express generosity or the greed to be good? Again, if generous acts are acts in which the good is freely given, why be generous? Why care about the welfare of others unless our own welfare is somehow wrapped up with theirs?

Atonement is one possibility. If the neediness of others results from, or is imagined to result from, damage we have done to them, then generosity towards them—the transfer to them of the good we have—can be considered a reparative act. This makes generosity an attempt to serve the neediness of others in order to purge ourselves of our identification with a bad self rooted in the conviction that we are the cause of their suffering, an identification that causes us considerable suffering of our own especially in the form of guilt. Because of this, it can be said that there is a transactional element in atonement, although the transaction is a complex one. We are generous because only by generous acts can we establish ourselves as a generous person and thereby purge ourselves of our identification with a bad self.

Perhaps we should not be so intent on purging generosity of its transactional component. Perhaps caring about others is always driven by the hope that by doing so we become worthy of being cared for ourselves. But there is a difference between caring for others because it elicits in them an urge to care for us and caring for others as a way of altering the standing of our selves *internally*. Penance is a good example of the attempt to care for others as a way of purging ourselves of our identification with a bad self and thereby relieving ourselves of a harsh internal voice so that we can achieve peace of mind.

Does this mean that our generosity is proportional to the intensity of our struggle against identification with a bad self? Is there no generosity that is simply a quality of character that makes us intrinsically good rather than bad? And, if not, are we really better off with this problematic—or as-if—form of generosity given its connection to the predominance of an identification with the bad self? If we do not think badly of ourselves, if we do not carry a powerful unconscious conviction that we are essentially bad (unworthy of love), can we still be generous?

We might be tempted to offer in answer to this question the observation that the good self is by definition a generous self, which is a self that is more concerned with the welfare of others than with its own interests. In other words, the bad self is the self-interested self. But that definition, even if true, does not help us very much since it leaves out any consideration of whether it is even possible for a self to be constructed in this way and still be a self. If we have a self and are aware of its presence, if we care about it, then having a self means that, at least to a significant degree, we will take an interest in it. And, further, our special closeness to it means that our interest in it is bound to be more real and pressing than our interest in others, especially those we do not know (strangers). Also, to the degree that we take an interest in the welfare of others, we are taking their selves as our end, which is a form of self-interest, although one built on projection of our self onto others. All of this does, however, suggest the following possibility: Our ability to be generous is not driven by our struggle with our identification with a bad self, but by our ability to suspend our interest in ourselves so that we can shift the object of our interest from self to other.

This observation might lead us back to the parental relationship and to the primary love that is essential to it. Primary love is all give and no take. What is given in primary love is something of value, arguably the most valuable of things. And, as mentioned in the previous chapter, it is arguable that primary love involves parents taking on a burden, especially an emotional burden. In this sense, it can be said to involve giving something that is of value to the one who is the source of the gift. So far as this is the case, the source of generosity is an identification with a good object, the object from whom we received primary love. This identification, then, becomes the source of our capacity to give to others without the expectation of a return. The question that remains is whether the object of generosity can become someone with whom we do not have a suitable connection. Even if it is clear that we can, through enactment with our children, recreate our original relationship, how can we transfer this dynamic onto strangers? Or, what does it mean to become a "generous person" and not just an emotionally competent parent?

As already suggested, the clearest response to these questions calls on our identification with our original source of primary love, which fosters a drive on our part to become that person. Having moved beyond the state of being defined by the receipt of primary love, we can only recreate the experience by taking on the role of its source rather than its object. But the fact that we cannot recreate this relationship as an adult does not mean that we give up hope we can rediscover it or renounce it as our goal in life. This means that there are two paths for us laid out by the quality of our original relationships. One involves a lifelong struggle to recreate the relationship with ourselves still in the original role of the one who receives. The other is to recreate the relationship with ourselves in the role of the parent who offers. These two paths are vital to understanding the meaning and possibility of concern for the welfare of others. Along one path lies a genuine concern for others, along the other lies the inability to conceive, let alone act on, any real concern for their well-being. Along the first path is the "vicarious enjoyment through identification" of the gratification originally available in our earliest object relations (G. Heilbrunn quoted in Akhtar, 2013, p. 54).

These two paths have something important in common: They both cope with the problem of other people and their needs by equating them with, or incorporating them into, archaic relationships as those have been internalized. One way to think about this rejects the idea that we ever relate to others as strangers, always as intimate acquaintances, always as reincarnations of those with whom we had our original intimate connections. As I have already emphasized, the internalized representation of early object relations is not a representation of them; rather it is real. And in the experience in the depths of the psyche in the here and now is the reappearance of the archaic objects, which have become real to us once again. These are not strangers. And, so long as our only way of conceiving others in the mind is as the incarnation of early objects, there are no strangers. This means that we relate to others *as if* we know them, even though we do not, because this is our only way of knowing them.

Pseudo-generosity

Pseudo-generosity is marked by the need to be generous. This need can have different sources, but two of special importance are: (1) the need to be perceived by others as generous, and (2) a powerful internal impulse to give to others what we value, in other words to be generous. This indicates not simply that we have the capacity to be generous in settings where that is important, but that we feel we *must* be generous if we are to achieve an emotional equilibrium. We have a powerful, indeed overpowering, impulse that must be released. Then, the purpose of our generosity is not so much to serve the needs of others as it is to relieve the internal pressure. On some level, we do not feel we will survive if we cannot be generous. Too much, if not everything, is at stake.

The need to which I have just referred can arise in different ways. It is possible, for example, that having the good things creates anxiety that can be relieved if we rid ourselves of them and pass them on to others who, unlike us, can find satisfaction in having them. And, even if they cannot, we can find relief in passing them along. There is, then, a secondary gain in doing so which is that passing along the good things possession of which causes us to suffer will establish our generosity and make a virtue out of what would otherwise seem a failing: our inability to find pleasure in possession and use of things of value.

It is possible that we cannot hold onto the good things because we feel we do not deserve them, or that our pleasure having them causes those who do not to envy us. This might be the case if we are too involved ourselves with envy and are attempting to relieve ourselves of it by denouncing any unsatisfied desire that could be relieved by the good things.

CHAPTER 11

Use of and need for strangers

Depending on strangers

Our ability to relate to strangers, and therefore possibly to depend on them, is our ability to relate not to presence but to absence, or more accurately, to the special kind of absence their presence represents. This is absence of the emotional significance of self and other. Taking this as our starting point, the answer to the question, why would we care about the welfare of strangers or they about ours, would be: We don't, and they don't, at least so long as they remain strangers to us.

While this assessment may seem inconsistent with the demands of connection associated with living with others, in its way it is not. Not caring about the well-being of others indicates that, while we do not love them, neither do we hate them. And this means that we pose no threat to them. It could be said, then, that security in a world of strangers begins not with their love for or caring about us, but with their not hating us or wanting to do us harm.

When we care about strangers, we treat them as incarnations of important objects that have been instantiated in memory and fantasy. This would seem to be Melanie Klein's way of thinking about the problem when she considers the importance of gratitude. Our ability to care about strangers, understood as our capacity for compassion, is an expression of our urge to see in them familiar objects, in other words to find that they are not strangers. This method has the effect of denying something important to strangers, which is what is unknown about them. The more we accept that they are unknown to us, the less they become objects for our compassionate connection. The end of the compassionate relationship is not to care for strangers but to overcome what makes strangers strange to us and assure that our world has no strangers in it.

By contrast, the greater the significance of absence in presence, the more emotional salience the possibility of being a stranger to another has for us. It is important to us, then, that strangers survive primarily because strangers represent the part or aspect of our being that is not already known: our unknown self that forms the basis for our self-formation process. The more emotional salience being unknown to others has, the more heavily invested we are in institutions and ways of life that secure the well-being of strangers and assure their presence in our world. While we may not have an emotional investment in people we do not know, we may have an investment in the institutions that assure the security of the unknown self.

Our investment in the survival of strangers and of ourselves as strangers can be considered the emotional starting point for thinking about rights, which are the legal and institutional instantiation of freedom. It is our access to negative capability and our experience of it as something positive in ourselves that underlies our ability to relate to and possibly depend on strangers. The security of our own capacity to exercise negative capability, then, depends on the security of strangers in our world. The exercise of negative capability is not secure unless it is safe to depend on and relate to strangers without negating what makes them strangers, which is absence. We need to be able to live with people we do not know, which means we need to live in a world in which we are unknown to others.

In order to identify more clearly the emotional significance of strangers, it will prove helpful to consider how the stranger fits into the distinction drawn by Winnicott between use of an object and relating to it. The distinction Winnicott attempts to draw hinges on the existence of objects independently of any emotional significance they have for us, in other words, their existence in their own right. Use is to be understood "in terms of acceptance of the object's independent existence, its property of having been there all the time." An object we can use "must necessarily be real in the sense of being part of shared reality, not a bundle of projections" (1971, p. 88). Winnicott emphasizes that, to use an object, the "subject must have developed a *capacity* to use objects" (emphasis in original), a capacity Winnicott considers "part of the change to the reality principle." According to Winnicott, this capacity "cannot be said to be inborn, nor can its development in the individual be taken for granted." Rather, the development of the capacity to use objects "depends on a facilitating environment" (p. 89).

If our capacity to use objects is an expression of our capacity to separate ourselves from them, then our capacity to live with and use strangers is an extension of the capacity to use objects. We use strangers because we need, or need to use, them. And we need to use strangers because our livelihood depends on our doing so. We also, of course, have the possibility of subsuming strangers into our subjective world, and, where we do not have a capacity to use objects, that is what we are likely to do. But, if we do have that capacity, then relating to strangers without undermining their being strangers to us is simply the extension of the use of objects to objects we do not know.

When we need to use strangers because our livelihood depends on them, this means that our livelihood depends on our ability to move objects outside the sphere of subjective or omnipotent control. The use of an object only works when those on whom we depend take on an important quality attributable to strangers: we relate to them without regard to their emotional core and its power to shape relating. Here, the language becomes awkward primarily because Winnicott does not consider using an object a form of relating. Because the normal use of the term relating includes, for example, exchange relations and workplace relating, it will be best to hold to the distinction between relating to an object as an emotional connection with it, and use as a form of relating in which the emotional connection does not play a part.

Use of others is what we do in everyday life with those we relate to in a professional capacity, or, at least, this is the goal in work settings, a goal instantiated, for example, in sexual harassment rules. The defeat of this goal begins with the feeling of significant discomfort in the use of objects and the urge to replace use with relating in Winnicott's sense. The important point is that, even if we do not relate to strangers in that sense, we need them, or need to use them.

Use of objects is only an important part of living when we live outside our circle of intimate relations, especially our family. In other words, Winnicott's idea applies not in general, but only to those ways of living where impersonal relationships are essential and where there is a special kind of living that takes place outside the boundaries of family life. Our capacity to use objects is all about both our capacity to tolerate living outside of those boundaries and our urge to be part of a life lived outside those boundaries.

When we move into the new world of dependence on strangers, we can no longer assume that our livelihood is secure because others care about us. In an important sense, in that world, we are on our own. The resulting insecurity of our livelihood is to some degree an inevitable part of the maturation process, which is a process within which the security of dependence on our parents gives way to self-reliance made possible by the development of the self into an adult person.

There is a "facilitating environment" appropriate to self-reliance different from the one Winnicott describes as relevant to the early stages of emotional development. Self-reliance is made possible by a complex system of interdependence of individuals shaped by a process within which freedom plays an important part to the extent that an emotional investment has been made in the capacity to choose and decide. Success in making use of the facilitating environment depends both on the strength of the personality and on the reliability of the system within which that personality must lead a life appropriate to it.

Because of the possibility, even likelihood, of failure both of the individual and of the facilitating environment appropriate to it, there is significant pressure on individuals and on the environment to move in the direction of earlier forms of dependence. This regressive pressure mirrors the impulse to transform strangers into friends, autonomy into dependence. And, indeed, survival of the adult form of interdependence relies on the possibility of regression when needed, typically regression back into the family, but also regression in the mode of connection to the external world. Survival in the adult world is survival of individuals none of whom are fully adapted to it and all of whom will need to regress at various times in their lives.

One form that the compromise responding to this necessity takes is the development of a system of entitlements that translates the primitive form of dependence into a world suitable to self-reliance by making the security provided in the primitive setting a matter of right in the adult world. As a matter of right, the acquisition of the things we need is assured by an act of will on our part. As a matter of will, it both does and does not require regression to primitive forms of relating. This is because right imposes a more primitive mode of relating on the connection to strangers: those we call on by right to provide us with the things we need.

Isolation

To the extent that we are limited in our capacity to use objects, we are likely to experience a world without relating, which is a world where we use objects, as a world in which we feel isolated and alone. Isolation here refers to our being left alone with our most problematic internal objects because there are no external containers available for them. Our strategy for coping with this is to make those who populate the "outside" world, and to whom it is appropriate to connect by using objects, into containers for our bad objects. But when, as was the case for many during the Covid-19 pandemic, the outside world was closed, we will find limited opportunity to use others as containers for our bad objects. The result is a special kind of loneliness.

As Winnicott emphasizes, it is possible to feel comfort in being alone when "the good internal objects are in the individual's personal inner world" (1965, p. 32). This comment indicates how we can integrate the problem of response to strangers, and the possibility of stranger anxiety, with the problem of isolation. Because we are alone when we are with strangers, our capacity to be alone determines whether we can tolerate being with strangers or must instead redefine them as projections of our internal objects.

The kind of loneliness that is difficult to tolerate reproduces an emotional state experienced early in life when caregivers were unavailable to help manage difficult emotions. To the extent that we enter into a world of strangers, loneliness of this kind will result if the conditions for it are already in place internally. This special kind of loneliness can be confused with the loneliness many felt during the isolation imposed by the pandemic because it prevented normal contact with family members and close friends. Both kinds of loneliness were in evidence at the time, though they were not clearly distinguished. One difficulty during the pandemic was in distinguishing the feelings of anxiety and loss attributable to it and the underlying feelings intensified but not caused by it.

In its way, the pandemic heightened awareness of the underlying problem posed by the necessity of living in that special facilitating environment defined by dependence on strangers. The pandemic made our dependence on strangers problematic most notably because it cast doubt on the capacity of the world of strangers, or adult facilitating environment, to make livelihood secure. This, then, cast the possibility of freedom from the predetermined life in doubt. By undermining confidence that freedom is a possibility, the pandemic diminished the quality of life in the most fundamental way. People can live without much freedom in their lives. But they cannot live well if living well means experiencing presence of being both when they are alone and when they are not.

References

Akhtar, S. (2013). *Good Stuff: Courage, Resilience, Gratitude, Generosity, Forgiveness, and Sacrifice*. Lanham, MD: Rowman & Littlefield.

Balint, M. (1969). *The Basic Fault: Therapeutic Aspects of Regression*. Evanston, IL: Northwestern University Press, 1992.

Bion, W. R. (1962). *Learning from Experience*. London: Heinemann.

Bion, W. R. (1967). Notes on memory and desire. *Psychoanalytic Forum, 2*: 271–280.

Bittker, B. (2003). *The Case for Black Reparations*. Boston, MA: Beacon.

Blade Runner (1982). Warner Brothers. Directed by R. Scott. Written by H. Fancher and D. Peoples. Based on the short story by Phillip K. Dick.

Blade Runner 2049 (2017). Sony Pictures. Written by H. Fancher and H. Green. Directed by Denis Vileneuve. Based on the short story by Phillip K. Dick.

Bollas, C. (1989). *Forces of Destiny: Psychoanalysis and the Human Idiom*. London: Free Association.

Capehart, J. (2019). No reparations check of any amount could substitute for an apology. *Washington Post*, August 15. https://beta.washingtonpost.com/opinions/2019/08/15/no-reparations-check-any-amount-could-substitute-an-apology/ (retrieved August 15, 2019).

Coates, T. (2015). The case for reparations. *The Atlantic*, June. https://the-atlantic.com/magazine/archive/2014/06/the-case-for-reparations/361631/ (retrieved June 14, 2019).

Coates, T. (2019). Read Ta-Nehisi Coates's testimony on reparations. *The Atlantic*, June. https:// theatlantic.com/politics/archive/2019/06/ta-nehisi-coates-testimony-house-reparations-hr-40/592042/ (retrieved June 24, 2019).

Davis, T. (2019). What is generosity? (And how to be a more generous person). *Psychology Today* [online]. https://psychologytoday.com/us/experts/tchiki-davis-phd (retrieved May 26, 2019).

Dick, P. K. (1968). *Do Androids Dream of Electric Sheep?* New York: Doubleday.

Drehle, D. von (2019). Trump's wall is child's play compared to Bernie Sanders's climate plan. *Washington Post*, August 23. https://beta.washingtonpost.com/opinions/trumps-wall-is-childs-play-compared-to-bernie-sanderss-climate-plan/2019/08/23/cfb69490-c5da-11e9-9986-1fb3e4397be4_story.html (retrieved September 1, 2019).

Drezner, D. (2020). Trump has handled the coronavirus the way he handles everything: Like a toddler. *Washington Post*, April 3. https://washingtonpost.com/outlook/trump-toddler-coronavirus-pandemic/2020/04/02/163f5c04-7435-11ea-85cb-8670579b863d_story.html (retrieved April 12, 2020).

Durkheim, E. (1897). *Suicide*. R. Buss (Trans.). London: Penguin, 2006.

Erikson, E. H. (1959). *Identity and the Life Cycle*. New York: W. W. Norton, 1980.

Fairbairn, W. R. D. (1958). On the nature and aims of psychoanalytical treatment. *International Journal of Psychoanalysis*, XXXI: 374–385.

Freud, S. (1930a). *Civilization and Its Discontents*. New York: W. W. Norton, 1961.

Frum, D. (2016) "I'm Still a Republican—and I'll Fight to Reclaim My Party." *The Atlantic*, July 1. http://theatlantic.com/politics/archive/2016/07/david-frum-gop/489779/ (retrieved January 21, 2019).

Gerson, M. (2018). The last temptation. *The Atlantic*. https://theatlantic.com/magazine/archive/2018/04/the-last-temptation/554066/ (retrieved May 11, 2018).

Green Party US (n.d.). *Green New Deal*. https://gp.org/gnd_full (retrieved August 18, 2019).

Hesse, M. (2019). Don't blame MeToo for ruining the most iconic kiss in history. The photo was never romantic. *Washington Post*, February 20. https://washingtonpost.com/lifestyle/style/dont-blame-metoo-for-ruining-the-most-iconic-kiss-in-history-the-photo-was-never-romantic/2019/02/20/dc6be22e-348c-11e9-854a-7a14d7fec96a_story.html (retrieved December 5, 2019).

Institute of American Indian Arts. https://iaia.edu/about/ (retrieved January 19, 2020).

Kennedy, R. (1993). *Freedom to Relate: Psychoanalytic Explorations*. London: Free Association.

Kernberg, O. F. (1976). *Object Relations Theory and Clinical Psychoanalysis*. New York: Jason Aronson.

Kernberg, O. F. (1986). Further contributions to the treatment of narcissistic personalities. In: A. Morrison (Ed.), *Essential Papers on Narcissism*. New York: New York University Press.

Klein, M. (1957). Envy and gratitude. Reprinted in *Envy and Gratitude and Other Works 1946–1963*. London: Karnac, 1993.

Klein, M. (1992). Mourning and its relation to manic-depressive states. Reprinted in *Love, Guilt, and Reparation and Other Works 1921–1945*. London: Karnac, 1998.

Kohut, H. (1977). *The Restoration of the Self*. Madison, CT: International Universities Press.

Kohut, H. (1982). Introspection, empathy, and the semi-circle of mental health. *Journal of the American Psychoanalytic Association, 63*: 395–407.

Levine, D. P. (2017). The isolation of the true self and the problem of impingement: Implications of Winnicott's theory for social connection and political engagement. In: M. Bowker & A. Buzby (Eds.), *D. W. Winnicott and Political Theory*. New York: Palgrave Macmillan.

Levine, D. P., & Bowker, M. (2019). *The Destroyed World and the Guilty Self: A Psychoanalytic Study of Culture and Society*. London: Phoenix.

Locke, J. (1690). *Second Treatise of Civil Government*.

Magnum Photos (n.d.). Master of the photo essay. https://magnumphotos.com/?s=W.+Eugene+Smith (retrieved December 7, 2019).

Merriam-Webster (2003). Merriam-Webster's Collegiate Dictionary. Eleventh edition. Springfield, MA: Merriam-Webster.

Museum of Contemporary Native Art (2019–2010). Visual Voices: Contemporary Chickasaw Art. Santa Fe, NM.

O'Hagan, S. (2017). W. Eugene Smith: the photographer who wanted to record everything. *The Guardian*, August 6. https://theguardian.com/artand-design/2017/aug/06/w-eugene-smith-photographer-record-everything (retrieved January 15, 2020).

Riviere, J. (1964). Hate, greed, and aggression. In: M. Klein & J. Riviere, *Love, Hate and Reparation*. New York: W. W. Norton.

Schumpeter, J. (1950). *Capitalism, Socialism, and Democracy.* 3rd edition. New York: Harper & Row.

Stein, H. (1994). *The Dream of Culture: Essays on Culture's Elusiveness.* New York: Psyche.

Stephenson, S. (2017). *Gene Smith's Sink: A Wide-Angle View.* New York: Farrar, Straus and Giroux.

University of Notre Dame College of Arts and Letters (2019). What is generosity?   https://generosityresearch.nd.edu/more-about-the-initiative/what-is-generosity/ (retrieved June 7, 2019).

Volkan, V. D. (1988). *The Need to Have Enemies and Allies.* Northvale, NJ: Jason Aronson.

Winnicott, D. W. (1958). The capacity to be alone. In: *The Maturational Processes and the Facilitating Environment: Studies in the Theory of Emotional Development.* Madison, CT: International Universities Press, 1965.

Winnicott, D. W. (1960). Ego distortions in terms of true and false self. In: *The Maturational Processes and the Facilitating Environment: Studies in the Theory of Emotional Development.* Madison, CT: International Universities Press, 1965.

Winnicott, D. W. (1962). Providing for the child in health and in crisis. In: *The Maturational Processes and the Facilitating Environment: Studies in the Theory of Emotional Development.* Madison, CT: International Universities Press, 1965.

Winnicott, D. W. (1965). *The Maturational Processes and the Facilitating Environment: Studies in the Theory of Emotional Development.* Madison, CT: International Universities Press.

Winnicott, D. W. (1971). *Playing and Reality.* London: Brunner-Routledge, 2001.

Winnicott, D. W. (1986). *Home Is Where We Start From.* New York: W. W. Norton.

Index